THE UPS AND DOWNS OF THE PREMIER LEAGUE

Scholastic Children's Books,
Euston House, 24 Eversholt Street,
London, NW1 1DB, UK

A division of Scholastic Ltd
London ~ New York ~ Toronto ~ Sydney ~ Auckland
Mexico City ~ New Delhi ~ Hong Kong

Published in the UK by Scholastic Ltd, 2008

ISBN 978 1407 10388 4

Printed in the UK by CPI Bookmarque, Croydon, CR0 4TD

2 4 6 8 10 9 7 5 3 1

CONTENTS

INTRODUCTION

The Premier League has now been around for over 15 years – and in this book you're going to find out all that's happened since the league began.

You'll read about every team that's ever appeared in the Premiership – such as...

- The teams that have always been in.
- The teams that have been in – then never been seen again.
- The teams that have been in, then out, then in again.

You'll read about some of the Premier League's heroes – and villains. Like…

- The penalty-taker who got his old club relegated.
- The star who demanded a transfer because he was missing his daddy.
- The goalkeeper who staged a sulking sit-in.

And you'll re-live some famous Premiership moments. Such as…

- The coffee-cup goal.
- The medal-chucker's madness.
- The bad boy's bum-baring.

As if all this isn't enough, there's also another batch of our famous *Foul Football* awards for those who've helped turn the Premier League into the most pulsating league in the world. For example…

THE "I'M NOT FEELING VERY WELL, MUMMY" AWARD…
Darren Anderton – who played for Tottenham Hotspur between 1992 and 2004 … sometimes. He was so often out injured that the other players gave him the nickname *Sick Note!*

So read on for your numero uno, number one, first-of-its-kind guide to the tip-top teams of the Premier League!

BOLD BEGINNINGS

The Premier League...

England's Premier League – otherwise known as the Premiership – came into being at the start of the 1992–93 season. It was a big, big change. Since 1888, the year English league football started, the top division had been known as the First Division.

So, why the change? And was everybody happy about it – or did some cry "foul"!

So that's what happened. The clubs in the top division formed their own league, writing a new set of rules which said that they could keep the pots of TV money for themselves and not have to share it with all the other clubs in the lower divisions. A new league needed a new name, of course...

...and the rest

Some things did stay the same – sort of.

Every season, the teams finishing at the bottom of the Premier League – usually the bottom three – were relegated to the league below. Confusingly, this one-league-below-the-Premier-League league has changed its name almost as often as a footballer changes his socks. And, just to keep up, the leagues below *them* have made things worse by changing their names too! Here's a summary of the name game:

Year	Top League	Next to Top	Next to Next to Top	Next to Next to Next to Top
1888–1891	First Division			
1892–1919	First Division	Second Division		
1920–1922	First Division	Second Division	Third Division (South)	
1923–1957	First Division	Second Division	Third Division (South)	Third Division (North)[*]
1958–1991	First Division	Second Division	Third Division	Fourth Division
1992–2003	Premier League	First Division	Second Division	Third Division
2004–date	Premier League	The League Championship	League One	League Two

[*]Except that this wasn't a 'next to next to next to top' division, it was an equal 'next to next to top' division. The teams were allocated geographically, to cut down on travelling.

Confusing, eh? And it'll get even worse if I write sentences like: *in 1993, Nottingham Forest were relegated from the top league to the next to top league and, in 2005, relegated again to the next to next to top league.*

So in this book I'm going to use the current names, with something in brackets to say what the league was called at the time. For example: *in 1993, Nottingham Forest were relegated from the Premier League to The Championship (First Div) and, in 2005, relegated again to League One.*

Phew!

The fabulous forty

From 1992 until the end of the 2007/08 season exactly 40 clubs have appeared in the Premier League. Here are those fabulous forty, with facts about how many seasons they've been in the league and when.

Notice that some of the names are in bold letters. That's to indicate that the clubs concerned were **founder-members** of the league: that is, they were one of the 22 clubs playing in that first Premier League season of 1992/93.

Team	Seasons	Dates in Premier League
Arsenal	16	1992/93 – date
Aston Villa	16	1992/93 – date
Barnsley	1	1997/98
Birmingham City	5	2002/03 – 2005/06, 2007/08
Blackburn Rovers	15	1992/93 – 1998/99, 2001/02 – date
Bolton Wanderers	9	1995/96, 1997/98, 2001/02 – date
Bradford City	2	1999/2000 – 2000/01
Charlton Athletic	8	1998/99, 2000/01 – 2006/07
Chelsea	16	1992/93 – date
Coventry City	9	1992/93 – 2000/01
Crystal Palace	4	1992/93, 1994/95, 1997/98, 2004/05
Derby County	7	1996/97 – 2001/02, 2007/08
Everton	16	1992/93 – date
Fulham	7	2001/02 – date
Ipswich Town	5	1992/93 – 1994/95, 2000/01 – 2001/02
Leeds United	12	1992/93 – 2003/04
Leicester City	8	1994/95, 1996/97 – 2001/02, 2003/04
Liverpool	16	1992/93 – date
Manchester City	11	1992/93 – 1995/96, 2000/01, 2002/03 – date

Club		Seasons
Middlesbrough	13	1992/93, 1995/96 – 1996/97, 1998/99 – date
Newcastle United	16	1993/94 – date
Norwich City	4	1992/93 – 1994/95, 2004/05
Nottingham Forest	5	1992/93, 1994/95 – 1996/97, 1998/99
Oldham Athletic	2	1992/93 – 1993/94
Portsmouth	5	2003/04 – date
Queens Park Rangers	4	1992/93 – 1995/96
Reading	2	2006/07 – 2007/08
Sheffield United	3	1992/93 – 1993/94, 2006/07
Sheffield Wednesday	8	1992/93 – 1999/2000
Southampton	13	1992/93 – 2004/05
Sunderland	7	1996/97, 1999/2000 – 2002/03, 2005/06, 2007/08 – date
Swindon Town	1	1993/94
Tottenham Hotspur	16	1992/93 – date
Watford	2	1999/2000, 2006/07
West Bromwich Albion	3	2002/03, 2004/05 – 2005/06
West Ham United	12	1993/94 – 2002/03, 2005/06 – date
Wigan Athletic	3	2005/06 – date
Wimbledon	8	1992/93 – 1999/2000
Wolverhampton Wanderers	1	2003/04

The super seven

Of those 40 clubs only seven have been ever-present: that is, not only were they founder-members in the Premier League but they're still there. Not once have they been relegated. Perhaps your favourite team is one of them?

Three of these super seven clubs – Arsenal, Chelsea and Manchester United – are so super that they've each been given chapters to themselves!

THE PREMIER LEAGUE TIMELINE

1992   The League begins. It is organized by the Football Association (FA) and sponsored by the brewing company Carling. For their money, Carling get the right to decide what the League's called whenever it's mentioned on the television: *The FA Carling Premiership*.

1993   Manchester United finish top of the 22 founder-member clubs who play in that first season. They are the first Premier League champions.

1994   The Premier League is big business and clubs who aren't successful have to find somebody to blame – like, their manager. Before, during and after the 1994/95 season ends, 13 clubs change their manager.

1995   To cut down on league matches (thus making time for more European games) the League shrinks from 22 clubs to 20. This is done by relegating four teams at the end of the 1994/95 season but only promoting two.

1996   On 3 April, Liverpool beat Newcastle 4-3. Newcastle had been leading 3-2 until two late goals were scored by Liverpool. The match, which virtually puts paid to Newcastle's hopes of winning the league, is later voted Match of the Decade on the Premier League's website.

1997 It's not enough to win trophies any more. Players vote for each other to win awards. The 1997 Young Player of the Year award is won by a baby-faced David Beckham.

1998 The foreign invasion is well under way, with both players and managers from other countries now flooding into the Premier League. Frenchman Arsène Wenger of Arsenal ends the 1997/98 season by becoming the first non-British manager to be in charge of the League champions.

1999 Manchester United end the 1998/99 season by winning a unique treble. Not only do they finish as Premier League champions, they win the FA Cup and the European Champions' trophy as well.

2000 It's the final season of Carling's sponsorship. They're being replaced by credit card company Barclaycard. TV presenters will now have to learn to call the league by its new name of *The Barclaycard Premiership*.

2001 On 15 December, striker Les Ferdinand opens the scoring for Tottenham Hotspur against Fulham and wins himself £10,000 for scoring the 10,000th goal in the history of the Premier League.

2002 A new award, *The Golden Gloves Award* is presented for the first time. It's for the season's top goalkeeper and is won by Jussi Jaaskelainen of Bolton Wanderers.

2003 The Premier League goes on tour. With TV games being watched by huge audiences in the Far East, the *Premier League Asia Cup* is held for the first time in Malaysia. It features Chelsea, Newcastle Utd, Birmingham City – and the Malaysian national team! It's now held every two years in a different Asian country.

2004 Another name change for the League as its sponsorship is taken over by Barclays Bank. It's now known as *The Barclays Premiership*.

2005 In the 2005/06 season, Arsenal striker Thierry Henry finishes as the top Premier League goalscorer, with 27 goals – one more than the 26 goals scored by the entire (relegated) Sunderland team!

2006 The Premier League's record transfer fee hits 30 million pounds when Chelsea buy Andriy Shevchenko from A.C. Milan. He scores 14 goals all season, which works out at over 2 million pounds a goal.

2007 Bad news for TV types. They've another name change to struggle with. Barclays decide that the league should be called *The Barclays Premier League*. The good news is that it's supposed to stay like that until 2010 at least.

2008 Replica kits are big business. Maybe that's why, for the 2007/08 season, all 20 Premier League clubs announce changes to their shirt

WE SHALL NOT, WE SHALL NOT BE MOVED

In this section we look at four terrific teams who have been ever-present Premier League performers.

Aston Villa

Here's valiant Villa's Premier League record. The table shows the team's position at the end of every season.

(Don't worry if your Premier League favourite is a different team: there are identical tables coming up for every other team – so your favourite is bound to be there!)

Year	92/3	93/4	94/5	95/6	96/7	97/8	98/9	99/00
Position	2	10	18	4	5	7	6	6
Year	00/1	01/2	02/3	03/4	04/5	05/6	06/7	07/8
Position	8	8	16	6	10	16	11	6

But if you *are* an Aston Villa fan you'll have seen from the table that your team has never really looked like dropping out of the Premier League.

That's the good news: the bad news is that Villa have hardly ever looked like winning it, either!

Their best season so far has been the Premier League's first, in 1992/93. That year, Villa were second – but a long way second. They finished ten points behind Manchester United. Since then, there's been little to get excited about. This was shown in July 2006, when an article appeared in the local newspaper moaning about the club chairman, Doug Ellis, saying that he was stingy and didn't care enough about Villa becoming a top club. Whose idea was it?

a) The fans'.

b) The players'.

c) The manager's.

25

THE HOW-NOT-TO-SUCCEED-AS-A-MANAGER AWARD...
David O'Leary. A week after the story appeared, O'Leary left the club.

Since then, Aston Villa have been bought by an American businessman named Randy Lerner. Villa fans will be hoping for great things – but must be worried about one of his early decisions: for the 2007/08 season a new club badge was introduced. Where once it said "Aston Villa", it now says just "AVFC". If he cuts back in other areas, Villa could be in trouble!

Everton

Year	92/3	93/4	94/5	95/6	96/7	97/8	98/9	99/00
Position	13	17	15	6	15	17	14	13
Year	00/1	01/2	02/3	03/4	04/5	05/6	06/7	
Position	16	15	7	17	4	11	6	

If season 1993/94 had turned out slightly differently, Everton wouldn't be figuring in this section at all. Going in to their final match against Wimbledon, they needed a win to ensure that they weren't relegated… and after 20 minutes they were 0-2 down! But a fantastic fight-back saw Everton run out 3-2 winners to save their Premier League place.

THE "I'M NOT SAYING THE REF WAS A CROOK, BUT" AWARD…

Joe Kinnear, Wimbledon manager. After a match during which his team had had a penalty given against them, and an appeal for one (for handball) turned down, cranky Kinnear said the referee, "definitely had the old Everton scarf round his neck."

Everton's goalkeeper that day was Neville Southall, a player who'd had plenty of strange jobs before becoming a professional footballer. As one of those jobs was as a dustbin man, he never worried if the fans yelled "rubbish" at him!

Not that they did. Southall was Everton's star goalkeeper between 1981-98. One of his best games was in the 1995 FA Cup Final, when Everton beat

Manchester United 1-0 to win the cup. What did super Southall do after the game was over?
a) Go home for a quiet night.
b) Go to the club party and dance on a table.
c) Go missing for two days.

Answer: a) Southall was famously not a party person. After tucking his medal in his bag, he said goodbye to everybody else and drove back home to Liverpool for a quiet night in.

Neville regularly got narked, though. In one game, against Leeds United, Everton were 0-3 down at half-time. Rather than sit in the gloomy changing room with the rest of the team, sulky Southall came out and sat down with his back against his goal post.

Southall played over 750 games for Everton – a record still to be beaten.

THE STRONGEST SPONSOR AWARD...
Everton – whose shirts carry the name of a beer named "Chang". It's made by a brewer in Thailand and Chang is a Thai word meaning elephant!

Liverpool

Year	92/3	93/4	94/5	95/6	96/7	97/8	98/9	99/00
Position	6	8	4	3	4	3	7	4

Year	00/1	01/2	02/3	03/4	04/5	05/6	06/7	07/8
Position	3	2	5	4	5	3	3	4

Liverpool certainly hold one record that will never be beaten: their top total of 18 First Division championships. Strange, then, that although they've never been out of the Premier League – never been out of the top eight, in fact – they've not yet won it either.

They've been in the top-three no less than six times, but their most recent triumphs have all been in cup competitions. In 2000/01, they won an amazing three cups: the FA Cup, the League Cup and the UEFA Cup. Two years later they won the League Cup again and, in 2005, picked up the biggest cup of the lot – the European Champions trophy.

In 2006 Liverpool won the FA Cup again, beating West Ham in a penalty shoot-out.

Two crucial goals in those last two games were scored by the team's captain, **Steven Gerrard**. He was spotted by Liverpool before he was ten years old! After joining them as a schoolboy he then proceeded to play relatively few games. Why not?

a) He'd injured his toe.

b) He was too short.

c) He'd grown too much.

Answer: c) Although a reasonable 1.73 m (5 ft 8 in) when he was 14, Gerrard grew greatly in one year – by a massive 10 cms (4 inches)! This gave him back problems for a while. As for answer a)...

THE BLACK-AND-BLUE-TOES-NOT GREEN-FINGERS AWARD...

Steven Gerrard – who also missed a few games after getting a garden fork stuck in his toe while digging in a patch of nettles.

Alongside Gerrard at Liverpool between 1996 and 2004 was ace striker Michael Owen. He, too, was 1.73 m (5 ft 8 in) – the difference being that that's where he stopped growing.

It didn't make the slightest difference. Mini Michael may have been short but he was sharp. During his time at Liverpool, Owen scored 158 goals in 297 games, and was Liverpool's top scorer every season from 1998 onwards.

As former England manager Sven Goran Eriksson said about him:

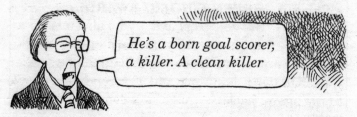

He's a born goal scorer, a killer. A clean killer

There's a Premier League goalscoring record that's held by a Liverpool player, though – and that player isn't Michael Owen. It's held by the striker he followed into the team, **Robbie Fowler**.

Fowler was Liverpool's star striker between 1992 and 2001, scoring 183 goals in 369 appearances (a few of which came when he returned to the club in 2006 for one season). And Robbie's record? Quick-footed Fowler is the scorer of the fastest-ever hat-trick in Premier League history. It happened during the second match of the 1994-95 season, when Liverpool beat Arsenal. See if you can match it in your next school game – but don't be in a hurry; you have to wait for 26 minutes before you get started. Then...

• Latch on to a defender's misplaced header and...

smack the ball into the net left-footed.

• Now take a pass on the left side of the penalty area, and...

hit a cross shot through a defender's legs and into the far corner of the goal for your second goal.

• Next, run on to a through pass and, as the goalie rushes out, try to clip it over him.

• This is the tricky bit. You don't manage it and the

ball shoots forward and looks like it's going out for a corner.

• Chase it, stop it with your left foot, pull it back a bit ...

then hit it into the net for your third goal!

• Check your watch. If scoring those goals has taken you longer than 4 minutes and 33 seconds you'll have to try again, because that's how long rapid Robbie took!

Tottenham Hotspur

Year	92/3	93/4	94/5	95/6	96/7	97/8	98/9	99/00
Position	8	15	7	8	10	14	11	10
Year	00/1	01/2	02/3	03/4	04/5	05/6	06/7	07/8
Position	12	9	10	14	9	5	5	11

The Premier League might not have started brilliantly for Tottenham in 1992/93, but at least their striker Teddy Sheringham went into the record books as... what?

a) The Premier League's first penalty-taker
b) The first top-scorer
c) The first hat-trick hitter

Answer: b) At the end of the season Sheringham topped the goalscorer's list with 22 goals.

Are you crazy about playing football, but think you're not fast enough at running? Don't worry about it. Sheringham was short of speed, too. He said:

I know I'm not quick, so I have to think quick

Tottenham's proud record of being a Premier ever-present looked very dodgy in 1994/95. They'd been found guilty of making illegal payments to their players. In addition to being fined and banned from the FA Cup for a year, they'd also been told that they wouldn't start the season with 0 points like all the other teams: they'd start with minus 12 points! In other words, they'd have to win four games to get to zero! In the end that part of the punishment was quashed and Tottenham went on to finish in seventh position with 62 points. But what would have happened if the 12-point ban had stood?

a) They'd have still come seventh.
b) They'd have finished lower, but not been relegated.
c) They'd have been relegated.

Answer: b) They'd have finished with 50 points, which would still have left them safe in 13th position, better than they managed two years later in 1997/98!

IT'S FROM TOTTENHAM; THEY'D LIKE A POINTS DEDUCTION EVERY YEAR, PLEASE

Rolling Robbie
In 2002, striker Robbie Keane joined the Tottenham team – and introduced their fans to one of the oddest goal celebrations ever seen. Do NOT try this in the playground unless it's made of sponge and covered with the softest of soft pillows … and even then, don't do it, because it looks really stupid.

1 Score a goal (that's the only non-stupid bit – Keane has hit nearly 100 for Tottenham).
2 Race towards the nearest corner flag.
3 Do a cartwheel.
4 When you land, do a forward roll.
5 Finally, pretend your fingers are a couple of six-guns and fire some shots.

THE AWFUL ARCHER AWARD...

Robbie Keane. After scoring a goal for his country, the Republic of Ireland, in the 2002 World Cup, rolling Robbie tried something different. Instead of firing imaginary six-guns he fired an imaginary arrow from an imaginary bow. Unfortunately he let both hands go at the same time – so that if he really had been holding a bow he'd have dropped it on his toe and the arrow would have gone nowhere!

Sometimes, though, the celebration would be given a miss. If Keane ever scored a goal against Coventry City, Leeds United or Wolverhampton Wanderers he didn't bother. Why not?

Answer: They were his former clubs and he didn't celebrate out of respect for the part they played in his career. Or, possibly, because he couldn't manage it any more. The player packed in his gymnastics at the end of the 2005/06 season.

I'D ADVISE A SIMPLE RUN BACK TO THE CENTRE-CIRCLE NEXT TIME, MR KEANE

THE TONGUE TWISTER AWARD...

Ossie Ardiles – the Argentine ex-player who was appointed Spurs' manager in 1993. He had trouble saying the club's name, which always came out as "Tottingham". Ardiles was sacked after just one year when it was decided that he may have been a great player but he was a rott*ing* manager!

THE NATTY NICKNAMES QUIZ

Every football club has a nickname. Some are natty, some are nifty – and some are no-brainers! Test your knowledge in this quiz featuring the nicknames of all forty clubs to have played in the Premier League by the end of 2007/08. Match the nicknames to their clubs...

1 COME ON, YOU COLOURS!

The real no-brain nicknames are those that are obviously related to the shirts the team wears – like these...

Nicknames: Blues, Hoops, Reds, Reds, Reds, Whites

Clubs: *Birmingham City, Leeds United, Liverpool, Manchester United, Nottingham Forest, Queens Park Rangers*

2 COME ON, YOU ABBREVIATIONS!

Another simple type of nickname is one that is a shortened, or slightly changed, version of the team's full name.

Nicknames: Boro, Dons, Hammers, Rovers, Saints, Spurs

Clubs: *Blackburn Rovers, Middlesbrough, Milton Keynes Dons, Southampton, Tottenham Hotspur, West Ham United*

3 COME ON, YOU MANGLES!

Sometimes a club's nickname is a mangled version of part of their real name.

Nicknames: Addicks, Citizens, Latics, Latics, Pompey, Villans

Clubs: *Aston Villa, Charlton Athletic, Manchester City, Oldham Athletic, Portsmouth, Wigan Athletic*

4 COME ON, YOU ANIMALS!

More adventurous fans have nicknamed their team after animals – maybe in the hope that it will inspire them to savage the opposition!

Nicknames: Black Cats, Foxes, Rams, Wolves

Clubs: *Derby County, Leicester City, Sunderland, Wolverhampton Wanderers*

5 COME ON, YOU FLYERS!

Another group of nicknames feature flying creatures – maybe because the fans hope their team will swoop on goal...

Nicknames: Bantams, Canaries, Hornets, Magpies, Owls, Robins

Clubs: *Bradford City, Newcastle United, Norwich City, Sheffield Wednesday, Swindon Town, Watford*

6 COME ON, YOU WORKERS!

All supporters like to see their team trying hard. Here's a group of nicknames based on jobs and work.

Nicknames: Baggies, Blades, Gunners, Singers, Tractor Boys

Clubs: *Arsenal, Coventry City, Ipswich Town, Sheffield United, West Bromwich Albion*

7 COME ON, WHEREVER YOU ARE!

Finally, here are six nicknames connected to the whereabouts of the club's ground.

Nicknames: Cottagers, Glaziers, Pensioners, Royals, Toffeemen, Tykes

Clubs: *Chelsea, Crystal Palace, Everton, Fulham, Leeds United, Reading*

Answers:

1 Blues (Birmingham), Reds (Liverpool, Manchester United and Nottingham Forest) and Whites (Leeds) are all boringly based on their colour. At least Hoops (Queens Park Rangers) is a little bit different: it refers to the style of the team's shirts – blue and white hoops.

2 Rovers (Blackburn), Boro (Middlesbrough), Spurs (Tottenham), Hammers (West Ham) and Dons (MK Dons – formerly Wimbledon) are just short versions of the teams' current names but The Saints (Southampton) is an abbreviation of their original name, St Mary's Young Men's Association FC.

3 Five of the nicknames come from manglings of the second part of the team's name: Villans (Aston Villa), Addicks (Charlton Athletic) and, likewise, Latics (Oldham Athletic and Wigan Athletic). Citizen (Manchester City) is also a dig at deadly rivals Manchester United, whose ground is actually outside the city of Manchester! Only Pompey (Portsmouth) comes from a mangling of the first word of the team name – maybe because it's the only word!

4 Black Cats (Sunderland) – a nickname which was adopted during the 1960s when the team's ground had a resident lucky black cat. Foxes (Leicester City) is a strange choice because the people who live in the area hate their animal! The nickname dates back to 1948 and was adopted because Leicestershire was famous for foxes and hunting. Rams (Derby) – a nickname which comes from a folk song, The Derby Ram. Wolves (Wolverhampton

Wanderers) is obviously, and rather boringly, an abbreviation of the team name.

I VOTE WE CHANGE OUR NICKNAME TO "BUNNY RABBITS"!

5 Five of this group come from the club's colours: Bantams (Bradford City, who play in black and amber), Canaries (Norwich, green and yellow), Hornets (Watford, yellow and black), Magpies (Newcastle, black and white) and Robins (Swindon, red). Owls (Sheffield Wednesday) is historic, though. It comes from the original name of Hillsborough, where Sheffield Wednesday play: Owlerton Stadium.

6 Baggies (West Bromwich Albion) is said to come from the protective trousers iron workers wore in that area of the Midlands; Blades (Sheffield United) because the city is the home of steel-making; Gunners (Arsenal) comes from the fact that the team used to play close to a weapons factory; Singers (Coventry) comes from the name of a bicycle-making company who were based in Coventry; Tractor Boys (Ipswich) refers to the farming for which the area is known.

7 Cottagers (Fulham) because their ground still has an old cottage – Craven Cottage – in one corner; Glaziers (Crystal Palace) refers to the original

Crystal Palace, a huge glass structure built for an exhibition in 1851; Pensioners (Chelsea) because the area's Royal Hospital is home to the famous red-coated Chelsea Pensioners; Royals (Reading) because the town is in Berkshire, not far from the royal home of Windsor Castle; Toffeemen (Everton) is usually said to have arisen because a toffee shop was close to their ground; and Tykes (Leeds United) simply because Leeds are a Yorkshire club and Yorkshiremen are tradionally known as "Tykes".

SUPER SIDES: CHELSEA

Chelsea's Premier League record

Year	92/3	93/4	94/5	95/6	96/7	97/8	98/9	99/00
Position	11	14	11	11	6	4	3	5

Year	00/1	01/2	02/3	03/4	04/5	05/6	06/7	07/8
Position	6	6	4	2	1	1	2	2

Chelsea highlights

Good Gullit and Rich Roman In the early years of the Premier League, Chelsea didn't have too many highlights at all. But when Dutchman Ruud Gullit became player-manager in 1996 things started to improve. Good Gullit began to import foreign players into the club – especially Italians. But it was the arrival of a non-Italian Roman that made the biggest difference: Roman Ambramovich, a mega-rich Russian. He paid the existing owner, Ken Bates, a whopping £140 million for the club – rather more than Bates himself had paid to buy Chelsea in 1982. How much was that?

a) £1

b) £100

c) £100,000

Answer: a) – although Chelsea were £1.5 million in debt, and Bates paid that off as well.

43

Champion Chelsea

Roman's riches paid off. After spending another £100 million or so on new players, in 2004/05 Chelsea raced to their first-ever Premier League title. They set loads of records on the way:

- Highest points total (95)
- Fewest goals conceded (15)
- Highest number of wins (29)

In 2005/06 they did it again! No records this time, although they did manage to equal their 29 wins.

Chelsea lowlights

In May 2006, Chelsea signed Ukranian striker Andriy Shevchenko from AC Milan for about £30 million – a record fee for a Premier League player.

Unfortunately, sharp-shooting Sheva turned out to be 'apless Andriy, at least in the 2006/07 season. Chelsea's hopes of winning the league for the third year running came to nothing when they finished second. As for Shevchenko's contribution, all he managed was a mere four league goals from 30 appearances!

Chelsea's main men

Italian striker **Gianfranco Zola** played over 300 games for Chelsea between 1996 and 2003, scoring 80 goals. Even though he was a bit of a titch (just 1.66 m tall, 5 ft 5 in) he was a big player. Zippy Zola was voted the 1996/97 Footballer of the Year. What was so special about this?

a) He was the first Chelsea player to win it.

b) No foreign player had ever won it before.

c) He'd only played part of the season.

Answer: a) ... and, never managed before by any player, c). Zola had missed the first three months of the season, having joined Chelsea in November 2006.

Many fans called him Gianfranco the Genius because of the amazing goals he scored. One of the best came in an FA Cup win against Norwich. Try it in your next school match:

• Wait until a corner is awarded on the right-hand side of the pitch. Then have one of your teammates pretend to be Chelsea's left-footed Graham le Saux.

• As he takes the corner and sends it swinging in a curve towards the goal, you start to run towards the ball.

• Here comes the tricky bit. When it reaches you, jump in the air...

• Let the ball go through your legs...

• Then back-heel it with the inside of your right foot into the corner of the net!

John Terry was Chelsea's captain during their two title-winning seasons. He's a rugged defender who scores goals. Just how rugged was shown during the League Cup Final of 2007 which Chelsea won. During the match, Terry was knocked unconscious and carried off to hospital. Having woken up, he insisted on being taken back to join in the celebrations – even though he couldn't remember playing in the game himself!

Terry was a crucial part of Chelsea's record-breaking defence in 2004/05, when they conceded only 15 goals. In 2006/07 tiger Terry had back trouble and was forced to miss a few games – during which Chelsea conceded another 15 goals: as many as they had in a whole season!

Jumping John isn't just a centre-back; he's played in goal for Chelsea, too. Only once, mind, taking over in a 2006/07 Premier League game against Reading when both Chelsea's regular goalkeepers were injured. How did he get on?

a) He took a free kick.

b) He didn't touch the ball.

c) He saved a penalty.

Answer: a) The game only had a minute to go, and that's all he did.

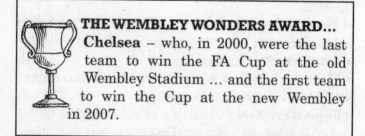

THE WEMBLEY WONDERS AWARD…

Chelsea – who, in 2000, were the last team to win the FA Cup at the old Wembley Stadium … and the first team to win the Cup at the new Wembley in 2007.

Chelsea quick non-players quiz

At Chelsea it's often been the people off the field who've made the most news. Try answering these questions about them.

1 Glenn Hoddle was Chelsea's manager from 1993 to 1996. Why did he leave?

a) He was sacked.

b) He was promoted.

c) He went off to manage another team.

2 Italian Claudio Ranieri, Chelsea's manager from 2000 to 2004, followed a policy of swapping his team around every week to give all his large squad of players a game. What was his nickname?
a) Change-io
b) Tinkerman
c) Revolvieri

3 José Mourinho became Chelsea's manager in 2004. What did he say at his first press conference?
a) We have top players.
b) We have a top manager, a European champion.
c) I think I'm a special one.

4 What nickname did the newspapers give Chelsea when they were bought by Russian billionaire Roman Ambramovich?
a) Chelsea Dynamo
b) Chelski
c) Coining-it-sea

5 After he'd received his medal as manager of the 2005/06 Premier League champions, José Mourinho threw it into the crowd of Chelsea fans. The league officials promptly gave him another one. What did he do with that?
a) Threw that into the crowd as well.
b) Gave it to his wife.
c) Sold it on an internet auction site.

Answers:

1c) ... and **b)** too, really. Hoddle left Chelsea to become England manager.

2b) – because he was always tinkering with the team.

3a), b) and **c)**! He also apologized if he was being arrogant!

4b) A good name for a team who were soon "Russian" up to the top of the league!

5a) – giving as his reason, "The medal was the same as the one I got last year. I didn't need another one, and I wanted to reward the fans for their support."

THE UNFAITHFUL FANS AWARD...

The lucky people who caught dozy Josés medals. They showed their love for Chelsea by immediately offering them for sale on the internet auction site, Ebay.

MADE IT AT LAST

There are three ways that a club can win promotion from the League Championship to the Premier League. They are:

1 Finish first

2 Finish second or ...

3 Finish 3rd, 4th, 5th or 6th and then go on to win a four-team knockout competition called "the play-offs".

None of these are particularly easy. Some clubs try it for years and years before they succeed. This chapter is all about teams like that...

Birmingham City

No. of Seasons in PL	5 (02/03–05/06, 07/08)
Highest Position	10 (03/04)
Lowest Position	19 (07/08) – R

Things had started pretty well for Birmingham. When the Premier League began in 1992, they'd just finished top of Division Three. That meant, with the leagues being renumbered, that they then vaulted straight to Division One!

THEY'RE GETTING READY TO VAULT STRAIGHT INTO THE PREMIER LEAGUE NOW!

Unfortunately, they didn't vault any higher for the next ten years – mainly because they kept on reaching the play-offs, only to fall flat on their faces! Here's Birmingham's rotten record:

• 1998/99 play-off: LOST to Watford in semi-final, 1-1 then 6-7 on penalties.

• 1999/00 play-off: LOST to Barnsley in semi-final, 2-5.

• 2000/01 play-off: LOST to Preston in semi-final, 2-2 then 2-4 on penalties.

Then, at last, in 2001/02, they actually won a play-off semi-final! After beating Millwall 2-1, they went on to play Norwich City in the final. At full-time the score was 1-1. Another penalty shoot-out! Would it be third time lucky for Birmingham?

It was! They won the shoot-out 4-2!

The team stayed in the Premier League until they were relegated in 2005/06. But they'd obviously got a taste for the top division because they bounced straight back again, winning promotion in 2006/07. No play-off performances this time, though. They finished second and gained an automatic promotion spot.

Fulham

No. of Seasons in PL   7 (01/02 – 07/08...)
Highest Position   9 (03/04)
Lowest Position   16 (06/07)

In January 1996, Fulham were almost as low as a team can get: out of the 96 teams playing in the Premier and Football Leagues they were in 95th place. Only Torquay United were below them. Could things get any worse? Yes, they could. When Fulham played Torquay that month, they lost!

Amazingly, though, that match was followed by a great revival. Fulham won enough games to avoid dropping out of the leagues altogether. Then...

- 1996/97 – they were promoted!
- 1997/98 – they were promoted again!
- 2000/01 – they were promoted once more, to the Premier League!

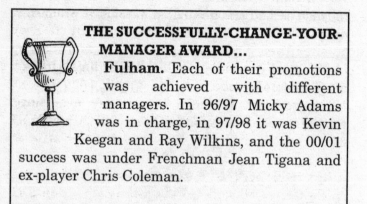

THE SUCCESSFULLY-CHANGE-YOUR-MANAGER AWARD...

Fulham. Each of their promotions was achieved with different managers. In 96/97 Micky Adams was in charge, in 97/98 it was Kevin Keegan and Ray Wilkins, and the 00/01 success was under Frenchman Jean Tigana and ex-player Chris Coleman.

At the end of the 2006/07 season, Fulham changed their manager again, appointing Northern Ireland manager Lawrie Sanchez. Did they follow their pattern of success in 2007/08? No! They only avoided relegation by goal difference and Sanchez got sacked!

Newcastle United

No. of Seasons in PL	16 (93/94 – 07/08...)
Highest Position	2 (95/96, 96/97)
Lowest Position	14 (04/05)

Most people (especially Newcastle fans) think that Newcastle have always been in the Premier League. Not so. They missed the first-ever season, only arriving in 1993/94 after being promoted the year before. That hadn't been in much doubt after they started with ten straight wins! And when they did arrive they carried on where they'd left off. They finished their first season in the Premier League in 3rd place – which is still the best finish by any newly-promoted side.

They've been a Premier League side ever since, coming close to being champions in 1995/96 and 96/97 when they finished both seasons as runners-up.

A hat-trick of Newcastle heroes

Andy Cole – who, in 1993/94, scored a stunning 41 goals in all games, and 34 in the Premier League. His reward: to be transferred! The manager Kevin Keegan sold Cole the Goal to Manchester United.

The Newcastle fans were seriously unhappy, and no wonder. Today, with around 200 goals to his credit for his various clubs, Andy Cole is the second-highest goalscorer in Premier League history.

THE UN'APPY ANDY AWARD ...

Andy Cole – and no, not because of his transfer. He was fed up with people calling him "Andy". In 2000 he announced that from then on he wished to be known by his proper name: Andrew.

Alan Shearer

Newcastle's fans cheered up again in 1986, though. Cole's place was taken by the first-highest goalscorer in Premier League history! In 1986 the club paid a then-record fee of £15 million to bring Alan Shearer from Blackburn Rovers.

Shearer's record goal tally in the Premier League is 260. During his 14 Premier League seasons he was top scorer three times, second three times, and fourth once. In the 1992/93 season he even managed fifth spot although an injury meant he didn't play a single game after Christmas!

When (go)Al Shearer eventually retired at the end of the 2005/06 season, he'd scored 206 goals for Newcastle in 303 games.

THE VERY, VERY, VERY EXPENSIVE MISTAKE AWARD...
Newcastle United – who, in 1985, rejected a 15-year-old striker when they had the chance to get him for nothing. His name: Alan Shearer!

THE VERY, VERY, VERY BAD DECISION AWARD...
Ruud Gullit – who was Newcastle's manager from 1998 to 1999. With Newcastle doing badly, he dropped Shearer for their match against deadly local rivals Sunderland. Newcastle lost the game 1-2 ... and, three days later, Gullit lost his job!

Not every Newcastle fan adored Shearer, though. Those in a film called *Purely Belter* certainly didn't. It was about two teenagers trying to raise money to buy season tickets. First they get him to sign autographs for them ... and then they steal his car!

Peter Beardsley

Peter Beardsley not only scored goals, he set them up for Cole and Shearer too. What's more, he loved Newcastle so much he signed for them four times! His first experience was a bad one: the club let Beardsley go when he was a teenager, just as they did with Alan Shearer. He came back for a second spell, this time leaving to join Liverpool. Back he came in 1993 and played so well in the Premier League that manager Kevin Keegan said:

The only way I'd substitute Peter Beardsley is if he got carried off. He can't be replaced. He's got everything

In 1997, off he went again. Finally, right at the end of his career, Beardsley returned for a fourth time to coach Newcastle's young players.

Portsmouth

No. of Seasons in PL	5 (03/04 – 07/08...)
Highest Position	9 (07/08)
Lowest Position	17 (05/06)

In January 2007, the football betting company Littlewoods produced a list of the most stressful clubs to follow – in other words, the teams that give their faithful fans a never-ending torrent of terrible torment. Only one club in the top ten was a Premier League outfit: Portsmouth. Look at this record and you'll see the reason why!

1992/93 – miss out on automatic promotion by goal difference (that is, the number of goals they'd let in subtracted from the number they scored), then lose in the play-off semi-finals.

1995/96 – avoid relegation to League One (then 2nd Div) by goal difference.

1997/98 – avoid relegation to League One by goal difference again.

1998/99 – avoid relegation to League One by goal difference yet again!

2000/01 – avoid relegation to League One by just one point.

While all this has been going on, Portsmouth have gone through six managers.

2002/03 – Portsmouth don't torment their fans with relegation battles or near-misses. Instead they give them heart attacks by winning the title and reaching the Premier League!

2004/05 – Portsmouth lose their manager, Harry Redknapp, to deadly local rivals Southampton. After flirting with relegation all season they finally scramble to safety with a 4-1 win over … Southampton! The fans nearly die with joy – not over Pompey's poor season, but because Southampton are relegated!

2005/06 – Redknapp returns, only to see the team go six games without scoring a goal.

2006/07 – After surviving the previous season with a late burst, Portsmouth finish in mid-table position.

2007/08 – Pompey finish in their highest position ever and win the FA Cup! Their fans agree all the stress has been worth it!

57

Matthew's missile

Fittingly, for a team whose mascot is a sailor, Matthew Taylor was Pompey's big gun. In season 2006/07 he scored a goal that couldn't have travelled faster if it had been fired from a cannon. Try it for yourself in your next school match. Here's how:

• Position yourself near the halfway line.

• Wait until the ball bounces high in front of you then, as it comes down, volley it ...

• So that the ball shoots into the air like a missile...

• Flies over the outstretched arms of the other team's startled goalkeeper ...

• And into the goal without touching the ground at all!

Reading

No. of Seasons in PL	2 (06/07 – 07/08...)
Highest Position	8 (06/07)
Lowest Position	18 (07/08)

Reading had to wait for a very long time before they finally won promotion to the Premier League. But, when they did, in 2005/06, they did it in style! At the end of the season they'd clocked up a record total of 106 points. But what sort of record was it?

a) The highest points total for a team promoted to the Premier League.

b) The highest points total Reading had managed in their history.

c) The highest points total ever accumulated by any team in any league.

Reading broke the record, previously held by Sunderland, on the last day of the season. They did it with a 2-1 win, thanks to a penalty scored by their captain Graeme Murty. It was his first goal for five years!

THEY'RE WORRIED HE'S FORGOTTEN WHERE THE GOAL IS !

When their first-ever Premier League season began, Reading got a mighty shock. Inside 20 minutes of their first game, against Middlesbrough, they were 0–2 down. But in a storming display they came back to win 3-2.

Wigan Athletic

No. of Seasons in PL	3 (05/6–07/8...)
Highest Position	10 (05/6)
Lowest Position	17 (06/7)

Not only were Wigan another team who thought they'd never make it into the Premier League, at one stage they thought they'd never make it into the football league! Nowadays the team winning the Football Conference League are automatically promoted to what is now called League two in place of the team which ends up at the bottom. But it used to be the case that the bottom teams, and any team which wanted to take their place, had to fill in an application form. The decision was then made by all the other league teams voting for the clubs they wanted. Wigan's application was rejected 34 times in a row!

They finally made it in 1977/78, but only really made their mark twenty years later. Even then, it seemed as if Wigan were doomed to failure. Three seasons in a row (1998/99, 1999/00, 2000/01) they reached the play-offs for promotion out of what is now League One (then 2nd Div) – and lost every time.

Finally, in 2002/03 they made it … and two years later were promoted again, to the Premier League.

Dogged Dave

A key figure in Wigan's success hasn't kicked a football for over 40 years. He's their chairman, Dave Whelan. He was a player with Blackburn Rovers and, in the 1960 FA Cup Final suffered the tragedy of being carried off with a broken leg. Not that long after, Whelan had to give up playing professional football. But dogged Dave bounced back. Instead of playing for a football club, he bought one instead! Having made a fortune from the JJB sports shops chain he'd built up, Whelan bought Wigan in 1995. Judging from their success since then, Whelan didn't just transfer lots of his money to the club but plenty of his doggedness too.

THE SPEND-YOUR-MONEY AWARD…
Dave Whelan – who not only has a large stake in JJB Sports, but also the JJB stadium where the two teams he owns, Wigan Athletic and rugby league team Wigan Warriors both play.

I THOUGHT IT WAS FOOTBALL THIS WEEK?

THE LATIN MOTTOS QUIZ

Having smart shirts bearing the club name and badge isn't enough for some clubs. They have to go a bit further and include a clever-dick motto which hardly anybody understands (especially the players!) because it's written in Latin.

Nine of these clubs are, or have been, in the Premier League. Here are their mottos – together with their translations into English. Unfortunately, the translations have been jumbled up. Can you sort them out? Match the right entry from column B with its partner in column A to discover the real club mottos – and if you struggle, nil desperandum (which means "don't despair")!

Club and Latin Motto	A	B
Blackburn Rovers Arte et Labore	By skill and...	1 excellence
Everton Nil satis nisi optimum	Nothing but the best is...	2 all things
Fulham Civibus et civitate	For citizens and...	3 courage
Manchester City Superbia in proelia	Pride in...	4 state
Tottenham Hotspur Audere et facere	To dare is...	5 good enough

Sheffield Wednesday Consilio et anamis	**Intelligence and...**	6 to do
Sunderland Consectatio excellentiae	**In pursuit of...**	7 industry
Swindon Town Salubritas et industria	**Health and...**	8 battle
West Bromwich Albion Labor omnia vincint	**Labour conquers...**	9 labour

Answers:

Blackburn Rovers – 9: *Arte et labore* means "by skill and labour".

Everton – 5: *Nil satis nisi optimum* translates to something like "nothing but the best is good enough".

Fulham – 4: *Civibus et civitate* means "for citizens and state" … which doesn't sound as though it's got much to do with playing football. That's probably because it hasn't! The motto was borrowed from the Borough of Fulham. The football club doesn't use it any more.

Manchester City – 8: *Superbia in proelia* means "pride in battle".

Tottenham Hotspur – 6: *Audere est facere* means "to dare is to do".

Sheffield Wednesday – 3: *Consilio et anamis* translates to "intelligence and courage".

Sunderland – 1: *Consectatio excellentiae* means "in pursuit of excellence".

Swindon Town – 7: *Salubritas et industria* means "health and industry".

West Bromwich Albion – 2: *Labor omnia vincit* means "labour conquers all things".

SCRAMBLING SPIDERS

Some clubs in the Premier League have climbed a bit, then dropped down, then climbed up again – a bit like footballing spiders, really!

Blackburn Rovers

No. of Seasons in PL	15 (92/3 –98/9, 01/2 – 07/8...)
Highest Position	Champions! (94/5)
Lowest Position	19 (98/9) - R

Blackburn are the spider-club who have climbed higher than any other: right to the very top of the Premier League! In 1994/95 they became champions. Spiders only have eight legs, but Blackburn's champion players had twenty-two ... and on the final day of that season every one of them was shaking. This is why...

• Blackburn were at home to Liverpool. Their nearest rivals, Manchester United, were away to West Ham. Man U could only become champions if they won and Blackburn lost. Any other results would mean the title went to Blackburn.

• The games began. Blackburn went 1-0 up. Man U's game was 0-0. The title was on the way!

• Gulp. Liverpool equalized. Blackburn's knees began to knock.

• In the last minute of the game, Liverpool won a free kick ... and scored again. Blackburn were losing 1-2. How were Manchester United getting on?

• On the Blackburn bench, manager Kenny Dalglish suddenly looked happier than any manager has ever looked after seeing his team concede a goal. He'd just heard on the radio that Man U's game had finished 0-0. Even though they'd been beaten, his team were Premier League champions!

THE NO AWARD AWARD...
David Batty – who was bought by Blackburn from Leeds United, only to promptly break his foot. He only played five games during the championship-winning season and so didn't get a winner's medal.

But after their triumphant year Blackburn began to slip – until, in 1998/99, they became the only former Premier League winners to have been relegated.

Spider-like, though, they scrambled back two seasons later. They haven't yet climbed back up to the top – but they're still in the Premier League, trying!

Charlton Athletic

No. of Seasons in PL	8 (98/99, 00/01–06/07)
Highest Position	7 (03/04)
Lowest Position	19 (06/07) – R

Most spiders like dark places, but Charlton Athletic play at The Valley. This ground has always been Charlton's home – except for a period of ten years in the 1980s when money problems forced them to leave and share a ground with Crystal Palace. During that period The Valley sprouted lots of grass.

The trouble was, much of it was in the stands where the spectators used to be!

The ground was finally reopened in 1992, the Charlton fans having helped with some of the early clearing by burning all the rubbish in the middle of the pitch! Now the players set about proving they *weren't* rubbish in the middle of the pitch. It took some time, but in 1997/98 Charlton scrambled into the Premier League by winning the play-off final against Sunderland.

A year later they'd slipped back again; but a year after *that* they'd scrambled back once more! And there Charlton stayed until 2006/07 when they slithered out of the Premier League once more.

THE YOUNG AND OLD LEFT-BACKS GO BACK AGAIN AWARDS...

Paul Konchesky and Chris Powell of Charlton Athletic. When precocious Paul ran out in August 1997 he became Charlton's youngest player at 16 years and 93 days; creaky Chris, on the other hand, was an ancient 31 years old when he won his first cap as left-back for England. He eventually moved to West Ham and played for them until he was replaced by a new left-back the club had signed ... Paul Konchesky! This meant that Charlton now needed a left-back, of course – so Powell went back there!

Derby County

No. of Seasons in PL	5 (96/97-01/02, 07/08)
Highest Position	8 (98/99)
Lowest Position	20 (07/08) – R

After making it into the Premier League in 1996/97, Derby stayed for six consecutive seasons until they were relegated in 2001/02. After that, they had a poor time and could well have been relegated again ... if, during their match against Nottingham Forest, they hadn't been saved by a coffee cup!

Here's what happened – and how to arrange for the same thing to happen when your school team are struggling. But be warned, it won't be easy!

• Before the game begins, lob a plastic coffee cup on to the pitch.

• Once the game's started, be ready for one of the other team's defenders to play a back pass to his goalkeeper.

• Now have one of your forwards – pretending he's Derby County's Paul Peschisolido – sprint into a goalscoring position.

• Here's the really tricky bit. You should have lobbed the coffee cup to the very spot on the pitch where the back pass is rolling...

• So that when the goalie runs out to kick the ball upfield it bounces over the coffee cup...

• Making the goalie miskick completely and pass it to your forward...

• Who scores!

Derby went on to win the game 4-2, and avoid relegation!

WE'RE TAKING NO CHANCES!

THE VERY NEARLY A. WARD AWARD...
A(shley) Ward – who, in 1997, scored Derby's last goal at their old ground, the Baseball Ground. He then thought he'd scored their first goal at their new ground, Pride Park ... until, 11 minutes from time, the floodlights failed and the match was abandoned!

IN THE DARK, THEY WON'T SPOT THE COFFEE CUPS!

GOOD THINKING!

In 2006/07 Derby didn't need any outside help, lucky or otherwise. They won the play-off final and scrambled back into the Premier League for 2007/08 – only to finish last with a record low of 11 points.

Ipswich Town

No. of Seasons in PL	5 (92/93–94/5, 00/1–01/02)
Highest Position	5 (00/01)
Lowest Position	22 (94/95) – R

Sometimes spiders get badly squashed. That's what happened to Premier League founder-members Ipswich Town in 1994/95. Every team seemed to be ready with a big boot – especially Manchester United.

They beat Ipswich 9-0! Poor old Ipswich even lost both games against their deadly East Anglian rivals, Norwich City. Not surprisingly, they were relegated at the end of the season.

THE "I DID MY BEST" AWARD...
Craig Forrest, Ipswich Town's goalkeeper. Even though he'd let in 93 league goals, the club's fans voted him their Player of the Season.

Climbing back into the Premier League proved to be really hard. For three seasons running, Ipswich were knocked out in the play-off semi-finals until they eventually made it in 1999/2000.

Once there, Ipswich almost spun their way to the top! They finished in fifth place. It didn't last. The following season they slithered down and out again.

Now it looks like history is repeating itself. They lost play-off finals in 2003/04 and 2004/05. But perhaps things will get better. Their current sponsor is E-on ... the energy company!

WHERE DO THESE IPSWICH PLAYERS GET THEIR ENERGY FROM?

Leicester City

No. of Seasons in PL   8 (94/95, 96/97–01/02, 03/04)
Highest Position   8 (99/00)
Lowest Position   21 (94/95) – R

Leicester have scrambled their way into the Premier League three times – and slid down the drainpipe and out again three times as well!

They've been in play-offs so many times it's a wonder they haven't been given a season ticket. In 1991/92 they missed the chance of becoming a Premier League founder-member by losing the play-off final. The following season they lost again. But the season after that, 1993/94, it was a case of third time lucky: Leicester won!

Unfortunately, they were immediately relegated. Back they scrambled and found themselves in yet another play-off final, against Crystal Palace. They won this game 2-1 – but left it a bit late. Their winning goal, scored by Steve Claridge, came four seconds before the final whistle!

THE TIRELESS LEGS AWARD...
Steve Claridge – whose 63 appearances for Leicester were just some of the 1,000+ games he played in a career that's taken him to over 20 professional and semi-professional clubs.

Leicester stayed in the Premier League for six years. In 2000/01 they even spun their way to the top for a couple of weeks. By 2001/02 things were looking good. A new stadium – sponsored by Leicester company Walkers Crisps – was almost ready to move in to. What a time for performances to snap! A disastrous season ended in relegation.

I WISH THEY WERE SPONSORED BY "RUNNERS CRISPS"!

But Leicester climbed back up again and the first season in their new stadium saw the team promoted to the Premier League once more. Once again, though, their legs weren't sticky enough to cling on and they were relegated.

Manchester City

No. of Seasons in PL   11 (92/93–95/96, 00/1, 02/3–07/8...)
Highest Position   8 (04/05)
Lowest Position   18 (95/96, 00/01) – R

After starting as founder-members of the Premier League, Manchester City dropped out at the end of the 1995/96 season. But in their case it wasn't a matter of scrambling up again: they kept on dropping! In 1997/98 they were relegated again, to what is now League One.

Back they came. Two successive promotions saw them return to the Premier League for 2000/01, only to drop out straight away. Back they climbed once more – this time to cling on. City have been a Premier League side since 2002/03.

Sharp-shooting Shaun

During this recent spell, one of their biggest players was Shaun Wright-Phillips – in spite of him being only 1.66 m (5 ft 5 ins) tall! A tricky winger with a powerful shot, he scored 26 goals for Manchester City before being transferred to Chelsea in 2005.

I SHOULD BE CALLED *SHORT* WRIGHT-PHILLIPS!

Middlesbrough

No. of Seasons in PL 13 (92/93, 95/96–96/97 98/99–07/08 ...)
Highest Position 7 (04/05)
Lowest Position 21 (92/93) – R

Middlesbrough are another side who have shown spiderish up-and-down form over the years. Although founder-members, their Premier League career started badly – they finished that first season second from bottom and were relegated!

They bounced back two seasons later, but clung on for only two more seasons before being relegated again in 1996/97.

THE WORST-SEASON-TO-BE-A-MIDDLESBROUGH-FAN AWARD...
1996/97 – a season in which their team were relegated, lost in the FA Cup Final to Chelsea, and lost in the League Cup Final to Leicester City. To cap it all their star player, Brazilian Juninho, was nominated for the Football Writers' Player of the Year awards – only to come second!

Back they came just one year later – and stayed. Middlesbrough have been in the Premier League since 1998/99. They've had little league success throughout that time, hovering around the middle of the table every season. But in that first year back Middlesbrough played a game that was anything but "pants"...

The Manchester Miracle
In December 1998, Middlesbrough travelled to Old Trafford to play Manchester United. Everything pointed to a Middlesbrough mauling. United hadn't

lost a Premier League home match for 18 months – and Middlesbrough hadn't beaten them for 68 years!

So hopeless did it look that a radio commentator and former Middlesbrough striker named Bernie Slaven promised that if Boro won he'd bare his bum in a department store window. And, when Middlesbrough pulled off the shock of the season with a 3-2 win, that's exactly what he did. With the scoreline painted across his cheeks he stood in the window to the cheers of the 2,000 fans who'd turned up to watch!

Norwich City

No. of Seasons in PL	4 (92/93–94/95, 04/05)
Highest Position	3 (92/93)
Lowest Position	20 (94/95) – R

Norwich City's spider-like qualities are rather

mixed. They're pretty good at climbing, but not so good at sticking around. History has shown that they're more like sliders than spiders!

As founder-members of the Premier League, Norwich started off really well, finishing 3rd in the League's first season. Then the slide began. The following year they came 12th. Things started to look better in 1994/95, with Norwich in seventh position at Christmas. But from then on the sliders couldn't have slid much faster if they'd been wearing greased boots. By the end of the season Norwich had fallen to 20th spot and were relegated.

Slowly, they climbed back. In 2004/05 they were a Premier League club once more. They had trouble keeping their feet again, though, and on the last day of the season Norwich needed a win away to Fulham if they were to have a chance of staying up. Sliding Norwich didn't win. They didn't draw. They didn't even lose by the odd goal. They lost 0-6!

Sheffield United

No. of Seasons in PL	3 (92/93–93/94, 06/07)
Highest Position	14 (92/93)
Lowest Position	20 (93/94) – R

Here's a Premier League riddle: why are Sheffield United like a light bulb? Because they always have bright beginnings and gloomy endings!

No team could have had a brighter beginning. Founder-members of the Premier League, Sheffield United's first game on the opening day of the 1992/93 season was against Manchester United. What record did they establish?

a) Scorers of the first Premier League goal.

b) First team to force a draw against Manchester United in the Premier League.

c) Hosts of the first floodlit Premier League game.

Answer: a) Sheffield United scored the opening Premier League goal with the season just five minutes old, and went on to win the match 2-1.

The following season, though, couldn't have had a gloomier ending. Needing a draw to guarantee survival, they were holding Chelsea 2-2 ... until, with the last kick of the 1993/94 season, Chelsea scored again to win 3-2 and send Sheffield United down!

81

Their return to the Premier League was a long time in coming, but they made it for the start of the 2006/07 season. How did they get on?

a) They scored the first Premier League goal of the season.

b) They were the first team to force a draw against Manchester United.

c) They were relegated on the last day of the season.

Answer: a)... and **c)** Yet again, Sheffield United started brightly by scoring the first goal of the Premier League season. And, again, they went into the final day needing a win – only to lose 1-2 to Wigan and be relegated.

West Ham United

No. of Seasons in PL	12 (93/94–02/03, 05/06–07/08...)
Highest Position	5 (98/99)
Lowest Position	18 (02/03) – R

West Ham climbed into the Premier League in 1993/94, just one season after the League began. They stayed put until 2002/03 – and might not even have qualified as a "spider" team if they hadn't lost some of their more famous legs:

• **Rio Ferdinand** left the club in November 2000, moving to Leeds United for what was then a record fee of £18 million; two years later he moved on to Manchester United for over £30 million!

• **Frank Lampard** walked away in May 2001, costing Chelsea £11 million.

THE "I WANT MY DADDY!" AWARD…

Frank Lampard – whose daddy, also named Frank, was assistant manager at West Ham until he left in 2001. Frank said after his transfer to Chelsea: "It would have been hard playing for West Ham without my dad there."

Even so, the West Ham spider still had plenty of famous legs. Their team for the 2003/04 season included:

• **David James** – goalkeeper in England's 2002 World Cup squad.

• **Trevor Sinclair** – winger in England's 2002 World Cup squad.

• **Joe Cole** – forward in England's 2002 World Cup squad.

• **Michael Carrick** – later to be picked for England's 2006 World Cup squad.

And yet they finished 18th and were relegated – which just goes to show that having good legs is no use unless they run around!

West Ham finally climbed back into the Premier League for 2005/06. Once there, they set about maintaining a record they'd rather do without. What is it?

a) They've always let in more goals than they've scored.

b) They've always been in the bottom half of the league at Christmas.

c) They've always lost on the opening day of the season.

Answer: a) Not once have West Ham ended a Premier League season with a goal difference greater than zero!

Even so, since their promotion they've managed to cling on – both to their League place, and to another Ferdinand. Performing in the West Ham defence has been Rio's younger brother, Anton.

THE VERY FORGETFUL BROTHERS AWARD...
Rio and Anton Ferdinand. In 2003, Rio of Manchester United forgot to take a drugs test and was banned for eight months. In 2007, a few days before an important game, brother Anton of West Ham went off to America with some friends to celebrate his birthday – and forgot to tell the truth. He'd told the club he was going to the Isle of Wight to visit his sick granny!

SUPER SIDES: ARSENAL

Arsenal's Premier League record

Year	92/3	93/4	94/5	95/6	96/7	97/8	98/9	99/00
Position	10	4	12	5	3	1	2	2

Year	00/1	01/2	02/3	03/4	04/5	05/6	06/7	07/8
Position	1	2	2	1	2	4	4	3

Arsenal highlights

Arsenal are the second-most successful team in Premier League history. They've been champions three times.

In **1997/98** they looked anything but champions. In the middle of the season they were 13 points behind Manchester United. One Manchester bookmaker was so certain about where the title was going that he didn't leave it until the end of the season to pay out winnings to those who'd bet on United! He started two months early, in March – only to stop when Arsenal travelled to Manchester and beat United 1-0. What's more, he had to pay out for a different team when the season did end. A fantastic unbeaten run saw Arsenal win the league with two games to go.

2001/02 was another title-winning season. What was the secret of Arsenal's success?

a) They scored in every game.

b) They didn't lose one match away from home.

c) They didn't lose one match at home.

In 2003/04, though, Arsenal were untouchable. They didn't lose a single game – home or away! Their 38 league games resulted in 26 wins and 12 draws. It was the first (and, so far, only) time a team has remained unbeaten throughout the whole of a Premier League season.

Arsenal lowlights

This unbeaten run continued into the following season, 2004/05 – until, by 24 October, it had reached a massive 49 games. That's when it was ended by Manchester United, 2-0 at Old Trafford.

That was only the start of things, though. The battle continued after the match was over. Sir Alex Ferguson, United's manager, complained that Arsenal players had thrown pizza and soup at him!

Arsenal's main men

Ian Wright was Arsenal's top striker from 1991 to 1998, so much so that when the 1997/98 season opened, he was getting close to the club's goalscoring record of 178 goals – prompting Wright to say:

"I'm five short – not that I'm counting."

He might well have been telling the truth. Counting wasn't one of Wright's strong points. When, on 13 September 1997, he banged in Arsenal's first goal in their match against Bolton Wanderers, Wright pulled up his shirt to reveal a T-shirt printed with:

179 Just Done It!

Unfortunately, he hadn't. He'd equalled the record, not beaten it. Fortunately, Wright's reckoning was up to the challenge of adding 1 to 178 – so when he scored again a little while later to beat the record for sure, out came the T-shirt again.

Thierry Henry broke Ian Wright's record – and didn't bother about a T-shirt. Signed by Arsenal in 1999, he hit a total of 214 goals altogether. Heroic Henry is also the holder of the Arsenal record for Premier League goals scored in a season (30), most goals scored in European matches (41) and most Champions League goals (35)! And, when the club ended their stay at their famous old ground, Highbury, he marked the occasion with a hat-trick!

Terrific Thierry may not have had a problem counting his goals, but Arsenal's fans could be forgiven for thinking that his memory wasn't that good. When Spanish club Barcelona tried to buy him in the summer of 2006 Henry heroically said:

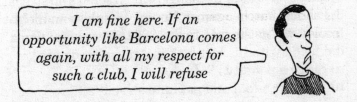

I am fine here. If an opportunity like Barcelona comes again, with all my respect for such a club, I will refuse

In the summer of 2007 Thierry Henry left Arsenal – and joined Barcelona.

YOU SAY YOUR MEMORY'S GETTING WORSE, EH?

DID I?

Arsenal quick quiz

1 By scoring 87 League goals for Arsenal between 1995 and 2006, Dutch player Denis Bergkamp showed he was a fearless striker. But what did terrify him?
a) Water
b) Spiders
c) Flying

2 Tony Adams spent his whole career with Arsenal, from 1984 to 2002. From 1988 he was Arsenal's captain. He played 504 games for the team ... but it could have been more if he hadn't missed three months of the 1990/91 season. Why?
a) He'd broken the law.
b) He'd broken club rules.
c) He'd broken his leg.

3 Patrick Vieira was a star in Arsenal's midfield from 1996 to the end of the 2004/05 season. What did he do with his last kick in Arsenal's colours?
a) Score a penalty.
b) Commit a foul and get himself sent off.
c) Score a winning goal.

4 After playing there since 1913 Arsenal left their famous old ground, Highbury, in 2006. How had they marked their final season at the ground?
a) By mowing the grass in a special pattern.
b) By wearing special shirts.
c) By having a "goodbye" song composed for them.

5 Arsenal's manager, Frenchman Arsene Wenger, was having trouble with two of his players. Dutch winger Marc Overmars and fellow Frenchman Nicolas Anelka were moaning about each other. How did Wenger sort out the trouble?
a) Put them in a boxing ring together.
b) Lied to them both.
c) Sold one of them to another club.

Answers

1c) A fear known as aviophobia. It began in 1994, when Bergkamp was with the Dutch squad and a journalist joked about a bomb being found on board their delayed plane. After that he'd only travel to away games by road or train; if he couldn't do that, then he didn't play.

THE SOUND OF MUSIC AWARD...
Denis Maria Bergkamp – who may have been concerned about flying but didn't care that in England his middle name was usually given to girls. Back home in Holland, Maria was quite a common second name for a Catholic boy.

2a) Adams had been caught drink-driving and spent three months in prison. He later confessed that he was an alcoholic and recovered to play brilliantly both for Arsenal and England.

THE SHORTS STORY AWARD...
Tony Adams. When he made his debut for Arsenal, at the age of 17, terrified Tony was so nervous that he ran out onto the pitch with his shorts on back-to-front!

91

3a) ... and **c)** The 2005 FA Cup Final against Manchester United ended in a penalty shoot-out. Vieira scored the deciding penalty to win Arsenal the cup.

THE NOT-SO-CLEVER-KICKS AWARD...
Patrick Vieira – whose record of being sent off nine times is the worst in the history of the Premier League.

4b) Rather than their usual red, Arsenal played the 2005/06 in claret shirts – the colour they'd worn when they'd first started playing at Highbury.

5b) Anelka didn't speak English, and Overmars didn't speak French. Wenger, who spoke both languages, told Anelka in French that Overmars thought he was a great player – then told Overmars in English that Anelka thought *he* was a great player. Problem solved!

IN THAT CASE, ASK HIM IF HE'LL LEND ME FIVE HUNDRED POUNDS!

THE HEROES AND VILLAINS QUIZ

Sometimes players are heroes, at other times they're villains. Often it depends who you ask! Check out these suspicious seven and decide whether they were seen as **heroes** or **villains**.

1 Mark Bright played for Sheffield Wednesday for five years, becoming their highest Premier League goalscorer. In 1993 at the old Wembley Stadium, he became a hero by scoring the goal which sent Wednesday into the Cup Final at the expense of their deadly rivals, Sheffield United. But what happened in March 2007, when he came back at the age of 44 to play at the *new* Wembley? Was Bright a hero or a villain?

2 Jürgen Klinsmann played brilliantly for Tottenham Hotspur between 1994 and 1995, scoring 21 goals in 41 games. When he left the club, chairman Alan Sugar said he was – what? Hero or villain?

3 Paul Ince, who played in the title-winning Manchester United side of 1992/93, had joined them in 1989. When his club's fans saw him in his new United shirt, was he thought of as a hero or a villain?

4 Vinnie Jones earned a reputation for villainy during his days playing for Wimbledon and others. At the end of his playing career, he went off to Hollywood and became a film actor. What sort of parts did he play – hero or villain?

5 Sol Campbell played for Tottenham Hotspur from 1992 to 2001. When he asked for a transfer, however, he said, that whoever he went to play for, it wouldn't be Tottenham's deadly rivals, Arsenal. Did the Spurs fans think he was a hero or a villain?

6 Having signed for Coventry for £4.5 million in August 1998, Croatian defender **Robert Jarni** brought his wife with him to watch his new team play in a friendly match. Two weeks later, as the result of a chat he's supposed to have had with Mrs Jarni and before he'd played a single game for Coventry, roving Robert was sold to Real Madrid!
a) Did the club view Mrs Jarni as a heroine or a villainess?
b) Was Robert Jarni seen as a hero or a villain?

7 At the start of the 2006/07 season, **David Unsworth** was a Sheffield United player. By the last game of the season he was playing for Wigan – against Sheffield United in a crunch match. Whoever lost would be relegated from the Premier League. Unsworth ended up as both hero and villain. But which team called him a hero, and which thought he was a villain?

Answers:

1 Hero. In a charity match between two teams of celebrities and former professionals, Bright became the first player to score a goal at the brand-new stadium.

2 Villain. Sugar thought Klinsmann hadn't been loyal to the club because he'd signed for two years but left after only one. He went on television and screwed up Klinsmann's shirt, saying he wouldn't use it to wash his car!

THE CHANGE-YOUR-MIND AWARD...
Alan Sugar – who, in 1997/98, signed up a new striker: Jürgen Klinsmann!

AND TO PROVE THERE'S NO HARD FEELINGS, I'VE GIVEN HIM HIS OLD SHIRT BACK!

3 Villain – because the club Ince was still with at the time wasn't Manchester United, it was West Ham United! He'd had the photograph done and gone off on holiday expecting the transfer to go through while he was away. But it hadn't – and, worse, a newspaper had printed the picture.

4 Villain. His early roles were all big-muscled hard-men with small brains. No surprise, really. Sam Hamman, Jones's chairman at Wimbledon, once described the player as a "mosquito brain"!

5 Hero when he said it, but **villain** when he finally moved … to Arsenal!

6a) Villainess. It was later alleged that she'd told jelly-legged Jarni that she wouldn't allow him to stay with Coventry.

b) Hero… of sorts. Coventry's dismay at losing the defender was outweighed by the fact that they sold him for £750,000 more than they paid – a good profit in just two weeks!

7 Hero to Wigan, **villain** to Sheffield United. Unsworth scored the deciding goal from the penalty spot to give Wigan a 2-1 win and relegate Sheffield United.

YO-YOS

In this section you're going to meet the teams whose performances have been a bit like a yo-yo: up, down ... up, down ... up, down...

Bolton Wanderers

No. of Seasons in PL	9 (95/6, 97/8, 01/2-07/8...)
Highest Position	6 (04/5)
Lowest Position	20 (95/6) – R

Towards the end of the 1990s, Bolton were going up and down so often it must have made their fans feel dizzy.

1994/95 – promoted to the Premier League for the first time.
1995/96 – relegated immediately.
1996/97 – promoted again, as Championship (then Division One) winners.
1997/98 – relegated again!

It was a time of strange coincidences, too. Bolton had sealed their successful 1996/97 season by winning the final game to be played at their stadium, Burnden Park. They'd been there for 102 years, ever since receiving their first visitors – Everton.

Come the 1997/8 season, which team does the Premier League fixtures computer send along for Bolton's first home game at their brand-new Reebok Stadium? Everton!

It wasn't a happy start for the new ground, though. On the final day of the season, Bolton had to do better than their relegation rivals to stay up. But while they lost their final match, their rivals drew. Bolton were relegated on goal difference and their rivals kept their Premier League place. And who were those rivals? Everton!

Bolton's yo-yoing finally changed in 2001/02. They fought their way back into the Premier League – and have stayed there ever since.

Crystal Palace

No. of Seasons in PL	4 (92/3, 94/5, 97/8, 04/5)
Highest Position	18 (04/5) – R
Lowest Position	20 (92/3, 97/8) – R

If prizes were awarded for yo-yoing, then Crystal Palace would win them for sure. They've been in the Premier League four times – and been relegated after just one season each time!

The signs were there in the first-ever Premier League season, 1992/93. Palace were relegated on the final day, after being beaten by Arsenal. To make them feel even worse, one of Arsenal's goals was scored by Ian Wright – one of their former players!

Back yo-yoed Palace in 1994/95, after just one season away, to have a year which ended with good news and bad news.

The good news was that Palace finished fourth from bottom. Yes, three teams were below them! But the bad news was that 1994/95 was the season the Premier League reduced its member clubs from 22 to 20 – by only promoting two ... and by relegating four! Crystal were shattered! Down they went again.

They were back, after winning the play-off final, for season 1997/98. By now the League had reverted to its usual three-up, three-down promotion and relegation system. All Palace had to do was repeat their previous performance and finish fourth from bottom. Do that and they'd be fine. They didn't – and they weren't. Poor Palace finished at the foot of the table and were relegated.

They stayed away for rather longer this time, not yo-yoing back into the Premier League until 2004/05 thanks to yet another play-off final win. Sadly, it proved to be the same old story and at the end of the season they went straight back down again.

Which all goes to prove that when it comes to yo-yo teams, the inmates at the Palace are kings!

 **THE DIFFERENT-MANAGER-BUT SAME-OLD-STORY AWARD...**
Crystal Palace – who, every time they've made it into the Premier League, have had a different manager to the previous time. But, then again, picky Palace have had no less than 17 managers since the League started in 1992!

Nottingham Forest

No. of Seasons in PL	5 (92/3, 94/5–96/7, 98/9)
Highest Position	3 (94/5)
Lowest Position	22 (92/3) – R

Nottingham Forest weren't so much founder-members of the Premier League as floundering members. At the end of the 1992/93 season Forest were relegated. They'd become the first team to finish bottom of the new league. In other words, the club had gone down in history!

Forest's final game of that season was also the final game in the career of their long-serving manager, Brian Clough. Although the team lost 1-2 to Ipswich, manager Brian had some cause to celebrate: Forest's goal was scored by his son, Nigel.

THE BRAVE DECISION AWARD ...

Frank Clark – Clough's successor as manager. One of the first players he sold after taking over his new job was ... Nigel Clough!

Nifty Nottingham yo-yoed straight back up, though, and stayed in the Premier League for the following three seasons until, in 1996/97, they came bottom once more and were relegated for the second time.

But the yo-yo effect worked again. Thanks to the terrific goalscoring partnership of their strikers Kevin Campbell and Pierre van Hooijdonk, Forest bounced straight back into the Premier League for 1998/99. Unfortunately, when the season began neither was playing for Forest. Why not?

a) Transferred
b) Injured
c) On strike

Answer: a) and **c)** During the summer, Campbell had been transferred. When he heard about this, a disgusted Hooijdonk went on strike!

The striking striker eventually returned to the team after some months, but it was too late. Forest were heading for relegation again. Worse, they ended the season in last position – thus completing an unwelcome hat-trick of three bottom spots in their relegation seasons. With all those bottoms, it's a wonder their fans didn't start calling them Notting-bum Forest!

Sunderland

No. of Seasons in PL 7 (96/7, 99/00–02/03, 05/06, 07/08...)
Highest Position   7 (99/00, 00/1)
Lowest Position   20 (02/3, 05/6) – R

Sunderland aren't just a yo-yo club ... they're a record-holding yo-yo club! Here are the fabulous facts.

1995/96 – win promotion to the Premier League.

1996/97 – get ready to move into their new ground, the Stadium of Light, by being relegated!

1997/98 – fail to yo-yo straight back up after losing the play-off final against Charlton in a penalty shoot-out. The match itself had finished 4-4, a record high-score draw.

1998/99 – making no mistake this time, Sunderland yo-yo into the Premier League by winning the Championship (Division One) title with a record 105 points.

I ALWAYS USE THIS FOR ADDING UP BIG NUMBERS

2002/03 – after four seasons, Sunderland set a record they'd rather not have: they're relegated with a record low points total for the Premier League – a measly 19 points.

2004/05 – two seasons later, they're yo-yoing up again...

2005/06 – then down again, breaking their own rotten record for low points while they're at it. This time they only collect 15 points. It's the worst performance by any English league club for over 70 years – until Derby beat it in 2007/08 by surviving!

AND I ALWAYS USE THESE FOR ADDING UP LITTLE NUMBERS

As if that isn't enough, in the same season Sunderland's record high-points score from 1999 is broken by promoted Reading.

2006/07 – Sunderland yo-yo back up yet again and end **2007/08** by surviving.

THE RECORD-SETTING OWNER AWARD...
Niall Quinn – who scored Sunderland's first goal after their move to the Stadium of Light. It obviously made the ground very special for him, because in 2006 nifty Niall led a group of businessman in buying the club! He's now chairman.

ONE-SEASON WONDERS

They've been, they've gone – and, so far, they've not been seen again. They're the one-season wonders...

ONCE UPON A TIME, WHEN WE WERE IN THE PREMIER LEAGUE – AND I DO MEAN ONCE...

Barnsley

No. of Seasons in PL	1 (97/8)
Highest Position	19 (97/8) – R
Lowest Position	19 (97/8) – R

Barnsley came and went in 1997/98 mainly because their defence had more holes in it than a string vest that's been attacked by hungry moths! By the end of the season they were second from bottom, having let in 82 goals – 11 more than the bottom club, Crystal Palace!

Here are Barnsley's seven worst results of the season and the teams that beat them. Use the clues to match the thumping with the opponent.

24 August	Lost 0-6 at home to … a team of pensioners!	A. Manchester United
20 September	Lost 2-4 away to … a Liverpool team	B. Southampton
23 September	Lost 1-4 away at … a place more famous for its tennis tournament	C. Everton
4 October	Lost 0-5 away to … a North London team	D. Chelsea
25 October	Lost 0-7 away to … a team nicknamed the Reds	E. Wimbledon
8 November	Lost 1-4 away to … a team of Saints	F. West Ham
10 January	Lost 0-6 away to … well, let's just say they hammered Bradford!	G. Arsenal

Answers: 24 August – lost 0-6 at home to Chelsea (nickname, *the pensioners*); 20 September – lost 2-4 away to Everton (*whose ground is in Liverpool*); 23 September – lost 1-4 away to Wimbledon (*more famous for its tennis tournament than its football team*); 4 October – lost 0-5 away to Arsenal (*who play in North London*); 25 October – lost 0-7 away to Manchester United (*the Reds*); 8 November – lost 1-4 away to Southampton (*the Saints*); 10 January – lost 0-6 away to West Ham (*the Hammers*).

Swindon Town

No. of Seasons in PL   1 (93/4)
Highest Position   22 (93/4) – R
Lowest Position   22 (93/4) – R

Swindon's only season in the Premier League is now but a distant memory for their faithful fans. Just as well, really. Not only did they finish bottom of the League, they also let in 100 goals – which is still the worst performance by any club.

There was one bright spot to Swindon's season, though: the way they performed against eventual champions Manchester United. Swindon were the only team to – what?

a) Stop United scoring against them on their home ground, Old Trafford.

b) Win a penalty against Manchester United.

c) Score four league goals against Manchester United.

Answer: c) They forced a 2-2 draw against them at home. Then, when they played the return match, Swindon banged in another couple of goals … though, unfortunately, Manchester United scored four against them.

THE HOPELESSLY ACCURATE PREDICTION AWARD...

John Gorman – Swindon's manager in 1993/94. After Swindon were relegated, he predicted: "We won't be in Division One (as it then was) for long." He was right, but not in the way he intended. Far from bouncing back, Swindon had another rotten season and were relegated again. No wonder the Swindon fans' nickname for their manager was "John Gormless".

Since then, though Swindon have had the occasional up, they've unfortunately had more downs. In 2006 they became the first ex-Premier League side to drop into the bottom division (League Two).

Watford

No. of Seasons in PL	2 (99/00, 06/07)
Highest Position	20 (99/00, 06/07) – R
Lowest Position	20 (99/00, 06/07) – R

Watford shouldn't really be in this section, because they've reached the Premier League twice. But as they were immediately relegated both times you could say they were twice as bad as any of the other one-season wonders!

Grim Graham

In 1999/2000, Watford's hopes were high. Graham Taylor, the manager who – between 1977 and 1987 – had taken them through from the (then) Fourth Division to the (then) First Division, was back in charge. Now he'd guided them into the Premier League. Was more success coming triumphant Taylor's way? Sadly not. After Watford had finished the season with seven points fewer than any other team, grim Graham resigned.

Baffled Boothroyd

When Watford returned to the Premier League in 2006/07, new manager Aidy Boothroyd couldn't have been more pleased. He joined Watford from Leeds United, and who had his new team beaten in the play-off final to win promotion? Yes, his old team Leeds United! Come the end of the season, baffled Boothroyd was struggling with good news and bad news. The bad news was that Watford had finished bottom and been relegated to the Championship. But the good news was that things would have been even worse if he'd stayed at Leeds: they'd just been relegated from the Championship to League One!

 **THE NON-PLAYER PLAYER OF THE YEAR AWARD...**
Ben Foster – who was voted Watford's Player of the Year for season 2006/07 ... even though he wasn't a Watford player! He'd been on loan from Manchester United all year!

West Bromwich Albion

No. of Seasons in PL	3 (02/03, 040/5–05/06)
Highest Position	17 (04/5)
Lowest Position	19 (02/3, 05/6) – R

To be strictly accurate, West Bromwich Albion shouldn't be in this section either. They can't be called one-season wonders because, like Watford, they've made it to the Premier League twice.

They *looked* as though they were going to be one-season wonders, though. After being promoted to the Premier League for the first time in 2001/02 they were immediately relegated. But back they bounced in 2004/5 to try again. This was the one-season wonder!

At Christmas 2004, West Bromwich were bottom of the league. This was awfully bad news. Never in the history of the Premier League had the club who were bottom at Christmas avoided relegation.

Come the last day of the season, in spite of a good run of form, West Bromwich were still bottom – but nowhere near as hopelessly bottom as they had been at Christmas. In fact, if they were to beat Portsmouth and the three teams above them all did badly, then they'd stay up.

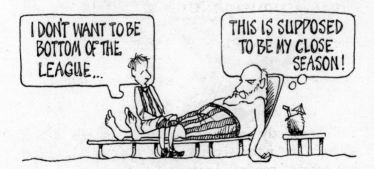

And that's exactly what happened. Instead of being one-season wonders again, West Bromwich could look back on 2004/05 as the one season when they left everybody wondering how they'd escaped the drop.

It was only the one season, though. They couldn't reproduce the trick in 2005/06 and were relegated.

Wolverhampton Wanderers

No. of Seasons in PL	1 (03/4)
Highest Position	20 (03/4) – R
Lowest Position	20 (03/4) – R

Wolves had one season in the Premier League, 2003/04 ... and it wasn't very wonderful.
• They lost their first match 1-5 away to Blackburn.
• They didn't score in their next five matches.
• They only won twice in their first 18 matches.
• They didn't win a single away game all season.
• They scored fewer goals than every other team.
That's why they finished bottom!

I SEEM TO HAVE LOST ALL MY BITE!

THE DING-DONG DERBIES QUIZ

Of all Premier League games, those against local rivals count the most. It may only be the same three points at stake, but boasting rights in school and at work count for much more! These games are known as "local derby" matches. But where did the phrase come from?

a) "The Derby", England's top horse race.

b) Everton and Liverpool, whose grounds were separated by a park owned by Lord Derby.

c) A village match played every pancake day in Derbyshire.

Answer: Possibly c), but probably a)

Nobody's too sure about the answer. The pancake day (Shrove Tuesday) match began over 800 years ago and is still held in the Derbyshire town of Ashbourne every year. It's a mad, rough game involving hundreds of players in two teams: the

"uppers", from one end of the town and the "downers", from the other end. One goal decides the game – which is harder than it sounds, because the two sets of goalposts are three miles apart!!

SINGLE TO THE OTHER GOAL, PLEASE!

The likeliest answer, though, is that the name came from The Derby – England's most famous horse race, started in 1780 by Lord Derby. Following this, a "derby" was often used as a name for any sporting contest. So a game between two neighbouring teams became a "local derby".

Wherever the name came from, it's a fact that local derbies are often foul affairs. Find out how foul by tackling (fairly, of course!) these savage seven questions!

1 Everton v Liverpool

Known as the Merseyside Derby, the games between Everton and Liverpool hold a special place in the history of the Premier League. That's because they've seen the most – what?

a) Goals
b) Sendings-off
c) Penalties

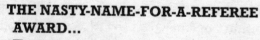

THE NASTY-NAME-FOR-A-REFEREE AWARD...

Everton supporters. In the 1999/2000 Merseyside Derby, referee Graham Poll cost Everton a win when he wrongly denied them a late goal. When he retired in 2007, Poll admitted to the Everton website that it had been a bad decision. The website was promptly inundated with e-mails, one of which said: "That's why we called him "Mr Liverpool"!

2 Newcastle United v Sunderland

Called the Tyne-Wear Derby, this match hasn't always been the friendliest of contests – as shown by what happened in 1996/97. What was it?

a) Newcastle banned Sunderland supporters from their ground.

b) Sunderland banned Newcastle supporters from their ground.

c) Both clubs banned the other's supporters from their ground.

3 Arsenal v Tottenham Hotspur

This game, also known as the North London Derby, was first played in 1887 – but the 2004 game was special. Arsenal were top of the Premier League and unbeaten. What happened?

a) Arsenal won 2-0.

b) Tottenham inflicted Arsenal's first defeat of the season.

c) The match was a draw.

4 Manchester City v Manchester United

According to Manchester City fans, this match shouldn't be known as the Manchester Derby at all. Why not?

a) Because the United club didn't begin in Manchester.

b) Because none of United's players were born in Manchester.

c) Because United's ground isn't in Manchester.

5 Portsmouth v Southampton

Known as the South Coast Derby, this game

had an extra ingredient of spice in 2004/05. Portsmouth's manager, Harry Redknapp, had left the club in December 2004 – and become manager of Southampton! A year later, which division was Harry's new team playing in? (Clue: Southampton were relegated at the end of the 2004/05 season.)

a) The Premier League
b) The Championship
c) Neither

6 Aston Villa v Birmingham City

Because both teams are based in Birmingham – which, after London, claims to be the most important city in England – this match is also known as the Second City Derby. It could be the number one derby for crowd trouble, though. A survey amongst Aston Villa fans conducted in 2006 revealed that 25% of them had witnessed fighting outside their ground.

In 2007, however, only 9% had seen trouble. What made the difference?

a) More police outside Villa Park.
b) Birmingham's fans had been prevented from travelling to Villa Park.
c) Lunchtime kick-offs, so that fans didn't spend all day drinking.

7 Chelsea v Fulham

Known as the West London Derby, this match had a controversial incident in 2006/07 when Chelsea's Didier Drogba had a goal disallowed for handball after the referee had discussed it with his linesman. This caused Chelsea manager, José Mourinho, to moan:

a) "It wasn't a handball!"
b) "Neither the referee or the linesman saw it!"
c) "I blame Fulham's players!"

Answers:

1b) – which makes it surprising that the match is sometimes referred to as "the Friendly Derby" (because Everton and Liverpool fans are often to be found in the same family)!

THE SCAREDY-PANTS AWARD ... **Bill Shankley, Liverpool manager (1959-74),** who, before the Everton team arrived for a derby match, gave a box of toilet rolls to the doorman and told him, "Give these to the Everton players when they arrive; they'll need them!"

2b) then **a)** – which makes **c)**! Because Sunderland's old ground wasn't very safe, they said Newcastle fans shouldn't come. In retaliation, when Newcastle were at home for the return match they'd didn't allow Sunderland fans to come. After that both sets of fans got together and formed a joint group to make sure the clubs didn't act so stupidly again.

3c) ... but it might have been **a)** Arsenal were 2-0 up before Tottenham equalized with a last-minute penalty. But they had the last laugh – the draw gave them the one point they needed to become 2003/04 Premier League champions.

4c) Manchester United's ground, Old Trafford, is outside the boundaries of the city – it's actually in Greater Manchester. United fans answer this taunt by pointing out that their club was formed in Clayton, which *is* in Manchester. And they began two years earlier, in 1878 rather than City's 1880.

THE WHO CARES, IT'S RESULTS THAT COUNT AWARD...
Manchester United. During the whole of the 1990s Manchester City didn't record a single win in the Manchester derby.

5 a) Southampton were no longer in the Premier League – but Redknapp was no longer with Southampton! He'd left them in November 2005, after just eleven months. His new team was his old team. Yes, he'd gone back to Portsmouth!

6 b – because Birmingham had been relegated the season before. The two teams hadn't played each other!

7 b), but especially **c)** The referee had initially given the goal, only to disallow it after appearing to agree to the Fulham players' appeals to talk to his linesman – who, Mourinho argued, wasn't in a position to see the offence anyway. Yes, that was the one thing that moaning Mourinho *didn't* complain about. He agreed that it *had* been a handball!

GONE BUT NOT FORGOTTEN

In this section we look at teams whose time in the Premier League is fast becoming a fading memory. Not only have they gone, they're showing little sign of coming back again...

Bradford City

No. of Seasons in PL	2 (99/00 – 00/1)
Highest Position	17 (99/00)
Lowest Position	20 (00/1) – R

Bradford City's two seasons in the Premier League were times of goodbyes:
• After City had just about hung on to their league place at the end of season 2000/01, manager Paul Jewell said goodbye to the club. He said he didn't think he could make the team any better than it was.
• His successor, Chris Hutchings, certainly couldn't. After the team won only one of their opening 12 matches in 2000/01, the club said goodbye to him. He'd been their manager for just 167 days!

SACKED? I HAVEN'T EVEN FOUND MY OFFICE YET!

120

• On 28 April 2001, Bradford City said goodbye to the Premier League. They'd been condemned to relegation by a 1-2 defeat against Everton ... after taking the lead, then missing two penalties!

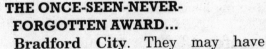

THE ONCE-SEEN-NEVER-FORGOTTEN AWARD...
Bradford City. They may have disappeared from the Premier League, but those who saw them play won't forget the experience in a hurry – especially if they'd left their sunglasses at home. Bradford City are the only professional team in England to play in colours of claret and amber.

Coventry City

No. of Seasons in PL	9 (92/3–00/1)
Highest Position	11 (93/4, 97/8)
Lowest Position	19 (00/1) – R

Not only were Coventry founder-members of the Premier League, they stayed around for its first nine seasons. It was always a struggle, though, with the team spending so much time just above the relegation zone that they should have been called "hover-try"! Here's their record over those nine seasons:
• 11th place – Twice
• 14th place – Once
• 15th place – Twice

- 16th place – Twice
- 17th place – Once

Finally, in 2000/01, they could only manage 19th spot and were relegated. They haven't been back to the Premier League since.

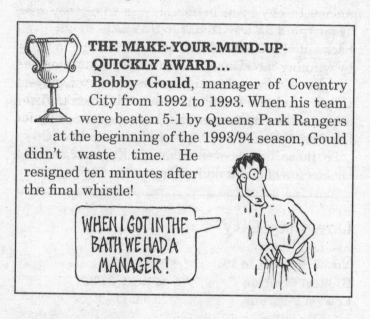

THE MAKE-YOUR-MIND-UP-QUICKLY AWARD...

Bobby Gould, manager of Coventry City from 1992 to 1993. When his team were beaten 5-1 by Queens Park Rangers at the beginning of the 1993/94 season, Gould didn't waste time. He resigned ten minutes after the final whistle!

WHEN I GOT IN THE BATH WE HAD A MANAGER!

Leeds United

No. of Season in PL	12 (92/3–03/4)
Highest Position	3 (99/00)
Lowest Position	19 (03/4) – R

Leeds were founder-members of the Premier League. More than that, they came close to winning it! They finished third once, fourth twice, and fifth four times.

What's more, in 2000/01, they reached the semi-final of the UEFA Champions League competition. That's when Leeds's troubles began – but they didn't have much to do with football.

After doing so well, Leeds then borrowed a lot of money to buy even better players than they had. Their thinking was that they'd be able to pay it all back out of the pots of money they expected to make by winning the Premier League and the Champions League and everything else with all the top players they'd bought. Unfortunately, they didn't. They slipped down the League, and didn't even qualify for the Champions League.

So there Leeds were, owing lots of money they couldn't pay back. All they could do was sell something. What?

a) Their manager
b) Their players
c) Their stadium

Answer: b) and c)! Selling top players like Rio Ferdinand and Jonathan Woodgate helped repay some of the debt. When that wasn't enough, Leeds sold their Elland Road stadium ... and their training ground! They then paid rent to play on them both every week.

(Leeds didn't sell their manager, David O'Leary. After he'd moaned about his best players being sold – and who could blame him? – he was sacked instead!)

Not surprisingly, from then on Leeds went from bad to worse. In 2003/04, after 12 seasons in the Premier League, they were relegated. In 2006/07 the team were relegated again. Nearly-leading Leeds had become mostly-losing Leeds.

Oldham Athletic

No. of Seasons in PL	2 (92/3–93/4)
Highest Position	19 (92/3)
Lowest Position	21 (93/4) – R

Oldham were in the Premier League for two seasons – and an eventful two seasons they were!

They were founder-members in 1992/93. With three matches to go Oldham looked doomed. They needed to win their games and hope other results went their way.

Amazingly, that's exactly what happened and Oldham survived to play in the 1993/94 Premier League season. They weren't doing too badly, either – and then they reached the FA Cup semi-final. That's when Oldham became fold-ham.

• With a minute to go in the semi-final against Manchester United, Oldham were leading 1-0 ... then United equalized to force a replay.

• They lost the replay, 1-4.

• Full of gloom, Oldham's League form suffered. They didn't win one of their last seven matches and were relegated.

Who knows how things would have worked out if Oldham had won that semi-final? As it is, Oldham's doldrums have lasted ever since. They haven't been able to climb back into the Premier League once.

Queens Park Rangers

No. of Seasons in PL	4 (92/3–95/6)
Highest Position	5 (92/3)
Lowest Position	19 (95/6) – R

Queens Park Rangers were founder-members of the Premier League. They lasted for four seasons before being relegated in 1995/96. The first three of those seasons, though, were pretty good: QPR finished 5th, 9th and 8th – mainly because they had an aristocrat in their team...

"Sir" Les Ferdinand

Les Ferdinand was nicknamed "Sir Les" by the Queens Park Rangers fans. Why? Because he was their top striker, banging in 90 goals for them.

OH, WELL, HE HAD A ROTTEN GAME LAST WEEK!

• In 1992/93 "Sir Les" ended as the League's second highest goalscorer with 20 goals.
• In 1994/95 he was the Premier League's third highest goal scorer, this time with 24 goals.
• In 1995/96, the year QPR were relegated, he once again finished as the Premier League's third highest goal scorer with 25 goals.

So what went wrong? Why did QPR go down, even though Sir Les's goal tally had gone up? Because that season he'd scored them for another club. QPR had sold him to Newcastle United ... and paid the price!

Les Ferdinand never returned to QPR. And they haven't yet made it back into the Premier League.

THE FAMOUS FOOTBALLING FAMILY AWARD...
The Ferdinand Family. Les Ferdinand is the uncle of both Manchester United's Rio Ferdinand and West Ham's Anton Ferdinand.

Sheffield Wednesday

No. of Seasons in PL	8 (92/3–99/00)
Highest Position	7 (92/3, 93/4, 96/7)
Lowest Position	19 (99/00) – R

Sheffield Wednesday played in the Premier League for the first eight seasons of its life. They obviously thought that reaching seventh place was heaven, because that was the best they ever achieved. Although Wednesday were relegated in 1999/2000, they never did sink to the very bottom of the League – which is more than can be said for one of their players...

THE BOTTOM OF THE LEAGUE AWARD #1...
Paulo di Canio – Sheffield Wednesday's mad Italian striker. Nicknamed "the volcano" by his then manager Ron Atkinson, potty Paulo was fined soon after joining the club ... for baring his bum to the crowd as a way of celebrating his first goal for Wednesday.

"THE VOLCANO" SHOWED HIS BUM? WHAT DID THE CROWD DO?

THEY ERUPTED!

Their final season in the Premier League was a disaster from start to finish. Wednesday were beaten 14 times in their first 19 games – and didn't score in ten of them.

Their bid to bounce straight back didn't start too well, either. Their goalkeeper, Kevin Pressman, began the new season by being sent off – after just 13 seconds!

Since then, Sheffield Wednesday haven't managed to fight their way back into the Premier League. But maybe they're the only English league club with a day in their name for a reason: they believe they'll return one day!

Southampton

No. of Seasons in PL	13 (92/3–04/5)
Highest Position	8 (02/3)
Lowest Position	20 (04/5) – R

For the whole of the 1990s, Southampton were the Premier League's great survivors. They spent nearly every season struggling to avoid relegation. When they managed to pull it off yet again, people wondered whether their nickname – the Saints – didn't have a ring of truth about it!

Here's a sample of Saints' scrapes:

1992/93 – avoided relegation by one point.

1993/94 – avoided relegation by one point.

1995/96 – avoided relegation by zero points! Saints survived on goal difference.

1996/97 – avoided relegation by one point.

1998/99 – after eight games, Saints had one point; they survived by winning their last three matches.

Magical Matthew

Matthew le Tissier was Saints' star player (some said their only player!) throughout this period. An attacking midfielder, it was magical Matt's regular supply of spectacular goals that made all the difference. So often did he come to Saints rescue that the fans nicknamed him – what?

a) Le God

b) The Guardian Angel

c) Saint Matthew

Answer: a) – probably because they spent every match praying that he'd score!

Here's an example of Le Tissier's talent. It's a goal he scored for Southampton against Newcastle in the first-ever Premier League season, 1992/93. Try it in your next match!

• You get a headed pass from your left-winger; but because it bounces behind you as you're running, you flick it forward with the back of your left heel.

• Now a defender's rushing at you! Flick the ball to one side of him as you run round the other side.

• Another defender's coming at you. This time, flick the ball up and over his head!

• You're into the penalty area. The ball's coming down again. As it lands, simply trap-pass it beyond the despairing goalkeeper and into the corner of the net!

Le Tissier had offers to move to other, bigger clubs, but spent the whole of his career with Southampton. He retired at the end of the 2001/02 season. Just three seasons later, without Le God to save them, Southampton were relegated.

Wimbledon

No. of Seasons in PL	8 (92/3–99/00)
Highest Position	6 (93/4)
Lowest Position	18 (99/00)

Wimbledon are unique amongst the clubs who have appeared in the Premier League. Why?
a) They've never had their own ground.
b) They no longer exist.
c) Their goal nets are used for hockey matches.

Answer: b), but with some **a)** and a tiny bit of **c)**!

Although they were founder-members of the Premier League in 1992/93, Wimbledon didn't play at a ground of their own; they shared a ground with Crystal Palace. After eight seasons as the worst-supported club in the League, during which they were always looking for a home of their own, Wimbledon were relegated in 2000.

In stepped a businessman from Milton Keynes who was looking to bring professional football to the town. So he bought the club, turned Milton Keynes'

National Hockey Stadium into a football ground – and put them together! At the same time, Wimbledon changed their name to Milton Keynes Dons (or MK Dons, for short).

LOOKS LIKE WE'RE CHANGING AGAIN!

None of this has helped the club get back into the Premier League. In fact, they've gone in the other direction. They were relegated again in 2003/04 and yet again in 2005/06 to reach the bottom division of the football league. One more drop and they'd have be known as MK Gones ... but in 2007/08 they finished as champions and were promoted back into League Two.

SUPER SIDES: MANCHESTER UNITED

Manchester United's Premier League record

Year	92/3	93/4	94/5	95/6	96/7	97/8	98/9	99/00
Position	1	1	2	1	1	2	1	1

Year	00/1	01/2	02/3	03/4	04/5	05/6	06/7	07/8
Position	1	3	1	3	3	2	1	1

Manchester United highlights

Manchester United's record is by far the best of any Premier League club. By the end of 2007/08 they'd won the title ten times, and they've never finished lower than third. But after just two games of the first-ever season in 1992/93, United's record was:

P	W	D	L	F	A	GD	PTS
2	0	0	2	1	5	-4	0

They were bottom of the league! But by mid-November they'd moved up to tenth place and, come the end of the season, they'd become the Premier League's first champions.

Here are the deadly details of United's other championship-winning years:

1993/94 – top of the League for all except the first two weeks of the season.

1995/96 – after losing their first game of the season with a team that features a number of young players – named Beckham, Giggs, Neville and Scholes – TV pundit Alan Hansen proclaims: "You never win anything with kids!" He should have added, "Well, apart from the Premier League title."

1996/97 – middle names are in, even if it does make you sound as though you play for rivals Arsenal. As they win the title again, United's top scorer is Swedish star Ole Gunnar Solksjaer – a player who, in 1999, would set a record by scoring four goals in 13 minutes in an 8-1 win against Nottingham Forest … after coming on as a substitute!

1998/99 – needing to beat Tottenham on the last day of the season, United go 0-1 down before picking themselves up to win 2-1 and become champions again. They follow it up by winning the FA Cup and the European Champions trophy to record an historic treble.

1999/00 – yawn… United lose only three matches and win the league by 18 points. Can any team challenge them next year?

2000/01 – it looks as though Arsenal can! The two teams are neck-and-neck – until they meet on 25 February ... and United win 6-1! A couple of months later, they become Premier League champions for the third season in a row.

THE YEAH-BUT-NO-BUT AWARD...
Sir Alex Ferguson, manager of Manchester United. At the start of the 2001/02 season he says it's his last one and he's going to retire. But by the end of the season – one in which United didn't win a trophy – he'd changed his mind. He was going to stay after all.

ERRR...

2002/03 – Ferguson's change of heart seems to give United heart. They win the League title again.
2006/07 – after three blank years, United become champions yet again ...
2007/08 – and again!

THE AWARDS AWARD...

Manchester United. At the end of the 2006/07 season, all the Premier League players vote for the players they think would make up the best team from them all. Out of the eleven players chosen, eight are from Manchester United.

WHERE DID WE GO WRONG?

Manchester United lowlights

It's difficult to find any lowlights for Manchester United – unless you call finishing third a lowlight! Season 1994/95 wasn't a fun one, though.

• They had their star midfield player, Frenchman Eric Cantona, banned for eight months for attacking a spectator who'd shouted nasty things at him after he'd been sent off.

• They drew their last game of the season ... when a win would have given them the league title.

• Then they lost the FA Cup Final, 0-1 to Everton.

Because of their success, if at any time Manchester United *don't* do well it's a cause for celebration amongst many football supporters. There are even special chants for Manchester United non-fans to join in with:

• Because United fans like to sing, *Glory, glory, Man.*

United, opposing fans will come back with *Rubbish, rubbish, Man. United.*

• United supporters (not unreasonably) have been in the habit of chanting, *Stand up for the Champions!* This is regularly changed to *Stand up, if you hate Man. U!*

Manchester United's main men

There was once a defender, a midfield player and a forward...

No, it's not the start of a joke – and Manchester United's opponents certainly haven't found them funny. Three of the team's star players during the Premier League's history have been defender Gary Neville, midfield player Paul Scholes and forward Ryan Giggs. What have they got in common?

a) They've all played for Manchester United and no other team.

b) They've all played over 500 games for Manchester United.

c) They've all got a full set of ten Premier League winner's medals.

Answer: a) and **b)**

All three played for Manchester United's youth teams in the early 1990s and went on to break into the full side. Since then, each of them has appeared more than 500 times for the club. Only one of them has the maximum ten winner's medals, though: Ryan Giggs. He was a regular first-team player in 1992/93; Neville and Scholes took another couple of years to get there.

Gary Neville, a marauding right-back, became club captain in 2005.

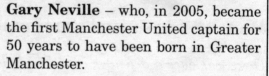

THE HOME-GROWN CAPTAIN AWARD...

Gary Neville – who, in 2005, became the first Manchester United captain for 50 years to have been born in Greater Manchester.

Not that long afterwards, he got into big trouble right at the end of a Premier League game against their deadly rivals Liverpool. When United, who had looked like losing the match, equalized in the last minute, Neville raced the length of the pitch to jump up and down in front of the Liverpool fans. He was fined £5,000, leading him to question whether the people running the game wanted humans or robots as footballers.

Paul Scholes, a midfielder who often

138

bangs the ball into the net, gets a regular mention from the Manchester United fans. One of their favourite chants is: Paul Scholes, he scores goals! But what does the player himself think about it?

a) He loves it.

b) He hates it.

c) He can't hear it.

Answer: b) Scholes prefers the quiet life and all the hoo-ha of being in the spotlight doesn't appeal to him at all. He once said:

> *I don't like talking about myself or being talked about. It's nice I suppose, but if I'm honest, I'd rather not be spoken about*

> SCHOLES IS FANTASTIC. PASS IT ON!

Ryan Giggs is Manchester United's long-serving star winger. Not only has he played in every one of United's title-winning teams, he's scored in every season – a record.

He was only 17 when he broke into Manchester United's first team. Soon everybody was talking about him. Nobody was talking *to* him, though. This wasn't because he wanted a quiet life, like Paul Scholes, but because Manchester United manager

Alex Ferguson wouldn't allow it. He was worried that the TV and newspaper reporters would demand too much of his time and wanted the young Ryan to concentrate on his football. Giggs wasn't allowed to give an interview for three years, until he reached the ripe old age of 20.

Waiting around wasn't something that rapid Ryan was used to. On 18 November 1995 he scored Manchester United's fastest-ever Premier League goal. See if you can reproduce the feat in the playground:
• Have the other team pretend to be Southampton, United's opponents.
• Start your stopwatch as the other team kick off...
• And pass the ball out to their left-wing ... where one of your players will win it.
• He (or she, of course) must now thump it towards the far side of the team's penalty area, where it's chested down by somebody pretending to be United's Eric Cantona.
• The alternative Eric waits for a moment, then passes it into the path of the player pretending to be Ryan Giggs...
• Who must half-volley it into the corner of the net!
• Stop your stopwatch and check the time.

Did your goal take longer than 15 seconds? Then go back and try again – because that's how quick Ryan's record goal was!

No wonder Manchester United fans sing (to the tune of "Robin Hood"):

Ryan Giggs, Ryan Giggs, running down the wing,
Ryan Giggs, Ryan Giggs, running down the wing,
Feared by the Blues,
Loved by the Reds,
Ryan Giggs, Ryan Giggs, Ryan Giggs.

Manchester United true or false quiz

1 Paul Scholes's favourite football team is Manchester United. **True or False?**

2 Star striker **Wayne Rooney** left school without a single GCSE to his name. **True or False?**

3 Fellow striker **Cristiano Ronaldo** was the most fouled player in the Premier League during the 2006/07 season. **True or False?**

4 Roy Keane, Manchester United's captain between 1997 and 2005 was often in trouble. During a derby against Manchester City in 2001 he was sent off for a foul that he'd been planning for four weeks. **True or False?**

5 Ryan Giggs is the only Premier League footballer to have been mentioned in the TV cartoon *Tom Jerry*. **True or False?**

Answers:

1 False – Scholes has admitted that his favourite team is Oldham Athletic, and that he'd quite like to play for them before he hangs up his boots.

2 True – but it didn't stop book publisher HarperCollins offering Rooney £5 million in 2006 for five books about his football life over the coming years. Not surprisingly, the only writing they expected from Wayne was his signature on a contract: the actual books are to be written by somebody else.

3 True – well, true if you believe Manchester United manager Alex Ferguson. After a match against Aston Villa in which Ronaldo was accused of diving to win a penalty, Ferguson insisted that Ronaldo was the most-fouled player in the league and definitely didn't fall down. In other words, Ferguson stood up for him!

4 False – according to the Football Association, he'd been planning it for four *years*! In 1997, Keane had been badly injured tackling a Leeds United player named Alfie Haaland. While Keane was flat out, awful Alfie had accused him of pretending to be injured. Four years later, with Haaland now playing for Manchester City, Keane got his revenge. As a result, he was fined and banned – not once, but twice! Firstly, for the red card; and then, secondly, when his autobiography came out and included a paragraph which made it sound as if he'd been planning the foul. The Football Association banned him for five games and fined him £150,000.

WHEN WE WERE AT INFANTS SCHOOL HE BORROWED MY PENCIL SHARPENER WITHOUT ASKING!

5 False – he's the only Premier League player to have been mentioned in *The Simpsons*. The episode was shown in November 2003.

THE FABULOUS FANS QUIZ

The Premier League teams wouldn't exist at all if there weren't hordes of fans raring to support them. And support them they do, with their chants and songs and … well, find out by tackling this quiz.

Each paragraph tells you something about the fans of ten teams. Complete the story by replacing the word FABULOUS with an item from this list:

Boing, Brazil, going down, Greasy Chip Butty, inflatable, marching in, play up, smoggies, the King, twelfth man, walk

1 Liverpool's fans must have the best-known anthem in football, with its rousing chorus of: "You'll never **FABULOUS** alone".

2 Arsenal's supporters devised a song to tell ace striker Thierry Henry how highly he was thought of – and not just at Christmas. Sung to the tune of the carol, The First Noel, it ends: "Thierry, Thierry, Thierry, Thierry; born is **FABULOUS** of Highbury".

3 Barnsley's time in the Premier League certainly impressed their fans – who, during matches would cry out: "It's just like watching **FABULOUS**!"

4 Manchester City's fans started a craze in the late 1980s. Forget replica shirts – they would turn up with bunches of **FABULOUS** bananas.

5 Portsmouth's rallying song is a simple thing called the "Pompey Chimes" – which goes, "**FABULOUS** Pompey, Pompey **FABULOUS**".

6 Sheffield United have an unofficial, and very unhealthy, anthem called: "The **FABULOUS** Song".

7 Southampton's supporters pinched a gospel hymn from the USA to sing to their team. It includes the line, "When the Saints go **FABULOUS**".

8 Norwich City were struggling in a 2004/05 Premier League match against Manchester City, so at half-time TV celebrity cook Delia Smith (the club's part-owner) stalked out on to the pitch and shrieked at the fans: "We need a **FABULOUS** here! Where are you?"

9 Swindon Town's fans were regularly taunted during the 1993/94 season with shouts from opposing supporters of: "**FABULOUS**, **FABULOUS**, **FABULOUS**!"

10 West Bromwich Albion have an internet fan magazine called, simply, "**FABULOUS**".

Answers:
1 Liverpool: "You'll never *walk* alone". It's nothing to do with football, though. It comes from a musical called *Carousel*, about a dead thief who's allowed back to earth for a day to help his daughter.

2 Arsenal: "Thierry, Thierry, Thierry, Thierry; born is *the King* of Highbury". Unfortunately for them, the club moved to their new ground shortly after – and "born is the King of the Emirates Stadium" didn't sound anything like as good!

3 Barnsley: "It's just like watching *Brazil*!" They may not have been serious. If they had been, Barnsley's stay at the top might have lasted longer than one season!

4 Manchester City: Their fans would turn up carrying bunches of *inflatable* bananas. Why? To show their support for one of their players, Imre Varadi, who they'd nicknamed Imre Banana.

5 Portsmouth: Sung to a tune that echoes the chiming of a clock, the fans sing, "*Play up* Pompey, Pompey *play up*". It began back in the 1890s – before Portsmouth themselves were formed. In those days the city's top team was Royal Artillery, who played

146

at a ground within earshot of the town hall clock. As it began to chime four o'clock, the time when games ended, the crowd would sing along with it.

6 Sheffield United: "The *Greasy Chip Butty* Song". It's a little song about all the things that make life worth living for a Sheffield United fan – such as local beer, chip sandwiches ... and, most of all, their football team.

7 Southampton: "When the Saints go *marching in*". Little do they know that in the USA it was usually played at funerals! As a coffin was taken to the cemetery, mourners would play or sing it slowly. Then, after the burial – to celebrate their belief that the dead person was now with the saints in heaven – play it joyfully.

8 Norwich City: "We need a *twelfth man* here! Where are you?" She was trying to stir the supporters into making more noise to encourage the team. Unfortunately, it fell as flat as a pancake. Norwich lost to a last-minute goal.

9 Swindon Town: As their team was stuck at the bottom of the League, the taunts were a very predictable, "*Going down, going down, going down!*" To their great credit, Swindon's fans would show their sense of humour by chanting back, "So are we, so are we, so are we!"

10 West Bromwich Albion's: internet fan-mag is called "*Boing*". It's named after the fans' tradition of bouncing up and down whenever the team scores a goal – though some opponents would say it's more like Albion's record in the Premier League: up, then down!

WHO ARE THE GREATEST?

Which team has been the most successful in the history of the Premier League? Which has been more derrière than premiere? This is where to find out! The table on the next page is based on every single Premier League match played between the League's opening day on 15 August 1992 and the final day of the 2007/08 season.

Where is your team? At the top? In the middle? Down in the relegation zone at the bottom? Perhaps they're not in the table at all, because they haven't yet been in the Premier League. That doesn't mean they never will be. In 2008/09 the fans of Hull City and Stoke City will see their teams playing Premiership football for the first time ever.

Wherever they are, keep supporting them. One of the great things about English football is that on their day, every team in the Premier League is capable of beating every other team.

All the ups and downs make it a truly pulsating Premier League!

WHAT A MATCH!

MY PULSE IS STILL PULSATING!

		P	
1	Manchester United	620	
2	Arsenal	620	
3	Chelsea	620	
4	Liverpool	620	
5	Aston Villa	620	
6	Newcastle United	578	
7	Tottenham Hotspur	620	
8	Blackburn Rovers	544	
9	Everton	620	
10	Leeds United	468	
11	West Ham United	502	
12	Middlesbrough	498	
13	Southampton	506	
14	Manchester City	430	
15	Bolton Wanderers	342	
16	Coventry City	354	
17	Sheffield Wednesday	316	
18	Wimbledon	316	
19	Charlton Athletic	304	
20	Leicester City	308	
21	Fulham	266	
22	Derby County	228	
23	Sunderland	266	
24	Nottingham Forest	198	
25	Portsmouth	190	
26	Ipswich Town	202	
27	Queens Park Rangers	164	
28	Birmingham City	190	
29	Norwich City	164	
30	Crystal Palace	160	
31	Sheffield United	122	
32	Wigan Athletic	114	
33	Reading	76	
34	West Bromwich Albion	114	
35	Oldham Athletic	84	
36	Bradford City	76	
37	Watford	76	
38	Barnsley	38	
39	Wolverhampton Wanderers	38	
40	Swindon Town	42	

W	D	L	For	Agst	Pts
394	137	89	1220	538	1319
332	168	120	1048	547	1164
310	168	142	977	606	1098
306	157	157	992	607	1075
229	188	203	781	724	875
240	152	186	844	718	872
223	165	232	839	847	834
220	145	179	752	656	805
211	167	242	758	808	800
189	125	154	641	573	692
173	126	203	591	699	645
153	146	199	593	682	602
150	137	219	598	738	587
129	120	181	487	579	507
106	95	141	394	492	413
99	112	143	387	490	409
101	89	126	409	453	392
99	94	123	384	472	391
93	82	129	342	442	361
84	90	134	354	456	342
79	74	113	305	378	311
67	62	99	251	331	263
69	61	136	250	394	268
60	59	79	229	287	239
62	47	81	220	257	233
57	53	92	219	312	224
59	39	66	224	232	216
52	56	82	198	255	212
50	51	63	205	257	201
37	49	74	160	243	160
32	36	54	128	168	132
35	24	55	116	162	129
26	13	37	93	113	91
19	33	62	96	184	90
22	23	39	105	142	89
14	20	42	68	138	62
11	19	46	64	136	52
10	5	23	37	82	35
7	12	19	38	77	33
5	15	22	47	100	30

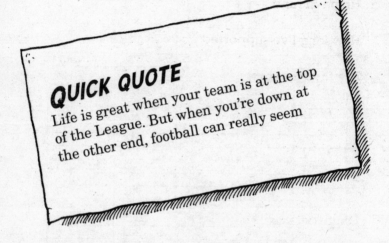

QUICK QUOTE
Life is great when your team is at the top of the League. But when you're down at the other end, football can really seem

MY TEAM

⚽⚽⚽⚽⚽⚽⚽⚽⚽⚽⚽⚽⚽⚽⚽⚽⚽⚽⚽⚽⚽

My football team

....

Team nickname

....

Home ground

....

How long I've supported my team

....

My fave players:

....

1.

....

2.

....

3.

....

Foulest player

....

Team manager

....

In 1988, replica kits went on sale in the shops for the first time. Now you could play for your favourite team in the park!

Number of matches I went to last season:

Home

Away

Best match ever

Best goal ever

Team stuff I own

Team stuff I'd like to own

Team website address

Team info number

Ticket office number

For the whole of the 1992 season, Arsenal kicked towards a North Bank packed with fans who didn't move and didn't make a sound! The ground was being rebuilt, and the fans weren't real – they'd been painted on a massive board behind the goal.

TEAM PRIZES

⚽⚽⚽⚽⚽⚽⚽⚽⚽⚽⚽⚽⚽⚽⚽⚽⚽⚽⚽⚽⚽

Cups won:

....

FA Cup

....

....

European Cup

....

....

UEFA Cup

....

....

League championships won:

....

....

....

....

....

....

Since the Villa side of the 1890s, no team pulled off the "Double" of winning both the League and the FA Cup in the same season until Tottenham managed it in 1960.

TEAM PREDICTIONS

⚽⚽⚽⚽⚽⚽⚽⚽⚽⚽⚽⚽⚽⚽⚽⚽⚽

What do you think is going to happen to your team this season?

Write down your predictions here, and check out if you're right in ten months' time...

....

What League position will they finish in?

....

What prizes will they win?

....

....

Who will be the top goal scorer?

....

Which players will leave?

....

....

....

....

Which players will join?

....

....

....

Between 1972 and 1991, Liverpool were either champions or runners-up in the League every year but one (the odd year out was 1980–81, when they finished fifth).

PERSONAL INFO

☺☺☺☺☺☺☺☺☺☺☺☺☺☺☺☺☺

Name

....

Nickname

....

Address

....

....

Telephone

....

Mobile phone

....

Email

....

Date of birth

....

Height

....

Weight

....

Boot size

....

Shirt size

....

Old football boots
(probably worn
to play against
the Romans!)

DAN FREEDMAN
THE KICK OFF

Jamie Johnson's got a score to settle

the **kick off**

DAN FREEDMAN

"You'll read this and want to get out there and play."
Steven Gerrard

"True to the game . . . Dan knows his football."
Owen Hargreaves

JAMIE JOHNSON'S DESPERATE TO BECOME HIS SCHOOL'S STAR FOOTBALL PLAYER (AND IN HIS DREAMS, A TOP PROFESSIONAL, TOO). HE'S GOT SO MUCH TO PROVE, AND NOT JUST ON THE PITCH - SO WHY AREN'T HIS MUM, TEACHERS AND BEST MATE ON HIS SIDE?

SHOOT TO WIN

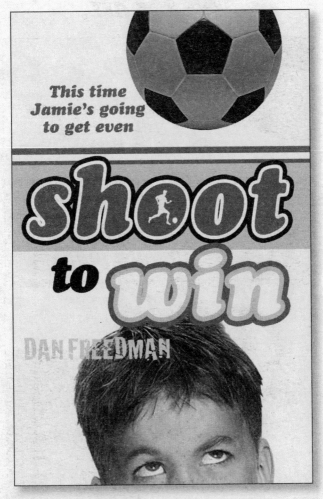

This time Jamie's going to get even

shoot to win

DAN FREEDMAN

JAMIE'S HOME LIFE MIGHT BE MESSY, BUT HE'S GOT A BIG MATCH COMING UP AND EVERYTHING TO PLAY FOR - SCOUTS FROM TOP CLUBS ARE COMING TO WATCH! BUT HIS NEW COACH IS BEARING A GRUDGE... HAS JAMIE MISSED HIS CHANCE?

AND DON'T FORGET TO LOOK OUT FOR JAMIE'S NEXT ADVENTURE, COMING SOON!

ARE YOU ON THE BALL?

FOUL FOOTBALL

KICKIN'
QUIZ BOOK

Michael Coleman

GUARANTEED TO FLUMMOX THE MOST FANATICAL OF FOOTBALL FANS,
THE KICKIN' QUIZ BOOK INCLUDES OVER 300 FIENDISH FOOTBALL
QUESTIONS, PLUS SCORES OF FOUL FOOTY FACTS.

FOOTBALL WITH THE FOUL BITS LEFT IN!